EYE ON
Art

THE AMERICAN ARTS AND CRAFTS MOVEMENT

by Barbara Sheen

LUCENT BOOKS
A part of Gale, Cengage Learning

GALE
CENGAGE Learning

Detroit • New York • San Francisco • New Haven, Conn • Waterville, Maine • London

LIBRARY OF CONGRESS CATALOGING-IN-PUBLICATION DATA

Sheen, Barbara.
    The American Arts and Crafts Movement / By Barbara Sheen.
        pages cm. -- (Eye on art)
    Summary: "These books provide a historical overview of the development of different types of art and artistic movements; explore the roots and influences of the genre; discuss the pioneers of the art and consider the changes the genre has undergone"-- Provided by publisher.
    Includes bibliographical references and index.
    ISBN 978-1-4205-0915-1 (hardback)
    1. Arts and crafts movement--United States--Juvenile literature. I. Title.
    NK1141.S54 2013
    709.73'09041--dc23
                                                            2013022294

Lucent Books
27500 Drake Rd
Farmington Hills MI 48331

ISBN-13: 978-1-4205-0915-1
ISBN-10: 1-4205-0915-2

Printed in the United States of America
1 2 3 4 5 6 7 17 16 15 14 13

CONTENTS

Foreword

"Art has no other purpose than to brush aside . . . everything that veils reality from us in order to bring us face to face with reality itself."
—French philosopher Henri-Louis Bergson

Some thirty-one thousand years ago, early humans painted strikingly sophisticated images of horses, bison, rhinoceroses, bears, and other animals on the walls of a cave in southern France. The meaning of these elaborate pictures is unknown, although some experts speculate that they held ceremonial significance. Regardless of their intended purpose, the Chauvet-Pont-d'Arc cave paintings represent some of the first known expressions of the artistic impulse.

From the Paleolithic era to the present day, human beings have continued to create works of visual art. Artists have developed painting, drawing, sculpture, engraving, and many other techniques to produce visual representations of landscapes, the human form, religious and historical events, and countless other subjects. The artistic impulse also finds expression in glass, jewelry, and new forms inspired by new technology. Indeed, judging by humanity's prolific artistic output throughout history, one must conclude that the compulsion to produce art is an inherent aspect of being human, and the results are among humanity's greatest cultural achievements: masterpieces such as the architectural marvels of ancient Greece, Michelangelo's perfectly rendered statue of *David*, Vincent van Gogh's visionary painting *Starry Night*, and endless other treasures.

The creative impulse serves many purposes for society. At its most basic level, art is a form of entertainment or the means for a satisfying or pleasant aesthetic experience. But art's true power lies not in its potential to entertain and delight but in its ability to enlighten, to reveal the truth, and by doing so to uplift the human spirit and transform the human race.

One of the primary functions of art has been to serve religion. For most of Western history, for example, artists were paid by the church to produce works with religious themes and subjects. Art was thus a tool to help human beings transcend mundane, secular reality and achieve spiritual enlightenment. One of the best-known, and largest-scale, examples of Christian religious art is the Sistine Chapel in the Vatican in Rome. In 1508 Pope Julius II commissioned Italian Renaissance artist Michelangelo to paint the chapel's vaulted ceiling, an area of 640 square yards (535 sq. m). Michelangelo spent four years on scaffolding, his neck craned, creating a panoramic fresco of some three hundred human figures. His paintings depict Old Testament prophets and heroes, sibyls of Greek mythology, and nine scenes from the Book of Genesis, including the Creation of Adam, the Fall of Adam and Eve from the Garden of Eden, and the Flood. The ceiling of the Sistine Chapel is considered one of the greatest works of Western art and has inspired the awe of countless Christian pilgrims and other religious seekers. As eighteenth-century German poet and author Johann Wolfgang von Goethe wrote, "Until you have seen this Sistine Chapel, you can have no adequate conception of what man is capable of."

In addition to inspiring religious fervor, art can serve as a force for social change. Artists are among the visionaries of any culture. As such, they often perceive injustice and wrongdoing and confront others by reflecting what they see in their work. One classic example of art as social commentary was created in May 1937, during the brutal Spanish Civil War. On May 1 Spanish artist Pablo Picasso learned of the recent attack on the small Basque village of Guernica by German airplanes allied with fascist forces led by Francisco Franco. The German pilots had used the village for target practice, a three-hour bombing that killed sixteen hundred civilians. Picasso, living in Paris, channeled his outrage over the massacre into his painting *Guernica*, a black, white, and gray mural that depicts dismembered animals and fractured human figures whose faces are contorted in agonized expressions. Initially, critics and the public condemned the painting as an incoherent hodgepodge, but the work soon came to be seen as a powerful antiwar statement and remains an iconic symbol of the violence and terror that dominated world events during the remainder of the twentieth century.

The impulse to create art—whether painting animals with crude pigments on a cave wall, sculpting a human form from marble, or commemorating human tragedy in a mural—thus serves many purposes. It offers an entertaining diversion, nourishes the imagination and the spirit, decorates and beautifies the world, and chronicles the age. But underlying all these functions is the desire to reveal that which is obscure—to illuminate, clarify, and perhaps ennoble. As Picasso himself stated, "The purpose of art is washing the dust of daily life off our souls."

The Eye on Art series is intended to assist readers in understanding the various roles of art in society. Each volume offers an in-depth exploration of a major artistic movement, medium, figure, or profession. All books in this series are beautifully illustrated with full-color photographs and diagrams. Riveting narrative, clear technical explanation, informative sidebars, fully documented quotes, a bibliography, and a thorough index all provide excellent starting points for research and discussion. With these features, the Eye on Art series is a useful introduction to the world of art—a world that can offer both insight and inspiration.

Introduction

Beauty and Simplicity

The Arts and Crafts movement is an art movement that developed in the mid-nineteenth century in England. It was characterized by simple, beautiful, and functional buildings, furniture, and decorative objects such as ceramics, lighting, stained glass, woodwork, and metal work. All elements were finely crafted by talented architects and craftspeople such as Frank Lloyd Wright, Gustav Stickley, Charles and Henry Greene, Ernest Batchelder, Dirk van Erp, Mary Chase Perry Stratton, and Louis Comfort Tiffany, among many others. The movement celebrated fine craftsmanship and the relationship between artists, their craft, and the environment.

Arts and Crafts Ideals

Arts and Crafts buildings, furniture, and decorative objects were designed in diverse styles using many techniques. Yet, a common group of ideals bound them together. These ideals included the belief that art comes in many forms, and the work of architects and craftspeople is as pleasing to the senses and has as much importance as that of painters and sculptors. Indeed, in 1882 when the British architect, designer, and early follower of the Arts and Crafts movement, A.H. Mackmurdo, formed a collective of designers known as the Century Guild of Artists, his goal was: "to render all branches [of architecture and the decorative arts] . . . to their rightful places beside painting and sculpture."[1]

Complementing this ideal was the concept that art should be a part of every person's life, not just that of the wealthy. As English designer and cofounder of the Arts and Crafts movement William Morris proclaimed: "I do not want art for a few any more than education for a few or freedom for a few."[2] Followers of the Arts and Crafts movement believed that every person could have art in their lives by living in a well-designed home decorated with finely crafted objects made by talented craftspeople.

The movement also encouraged amateurs to create works of art at home by practicing crafts like weaving, woodworking, and embroidering, just as people had in earlier times. British architect J.D. Sedding urged people to "take your crafts home, let them make your home homelier, family-life brighter."[3]

The movement rejected low-quality, mass-produced objects. It also scorned collections of useless knick-knacks, which were popular at the time. Replacing these items with simple, useful, finely crafted items was the way to create an art-filled home. "Have nothing in your house that you do not know to be useful, or believe to be beautiful,"[4] Morris insisted. According to U.S. architect and designer, Henry Mather Greene, "The idea was to eliminate everything unnecessary, to make the whole as direct and simple as possible, but always with the beautiful in mind as the first goal."[5]

Beauty, simplicity, unity of design, and harmony with the environment were essential to the philosophy of the movement. Architects, designers, and craftspeople used local resources for materials and were inspired by the local landscape. Their designs reflected nature and blended with the environment. Architects who believed in the ideals of the movement strove to create buildings that blended with their surroundings. For example, rather than build a skyscraper in the middle of the prairies

by hammer and hand do all things stand

Handcrafted wood-work, soft lighting, and a simple, clean design are all present in this example of an early 1900s Arts and Crafts home.

or a mountain chalet at the shore, Arts and Crafts architects designed low-slung ranch style homes in the prairies and informal bungalows at the shore. This was known as fidelity to place and helped to connect the home, the residents, and nature. This connection with nature was further enhanced by the use of large windows and porches.

In addition, the design of the building, furniture, woodwork, tile work, lighting, and decorative accents harmonized to create a serene haven in which families could thrive. As writer Ken Lonsinger explains: "The perfect home would complement the environment and provide a space to cultivate inner peace. . . . It is this theme, above all, that was the inspiration for beautiful architecture and design that still speaks to us today."[6]

The Movement's Timeless Principles

The popularity of the Arts and Crafts movement declined with the start of World War I (1914–18). Although it was replaced by newer artistic trends, the ideals and innovations of the Arts and Crafts movement still apply today. In fact, many modern people embrace Arts and Crafts principles and the lifestyle the movement advocated without even knowing it. For example, handcrafted items are still prized today. They are widely accepted as unique and superior to mass-produced items. Craft fairs featuring handmade stained glass, textiles, pottery, metal work, wood carvings, and pottery are very popular. Whereas mass produced items are often considered disposable, handcrafted items are prized and passed down in families. Decorative items made of natural materials like solid wood are considered by many people to be more beautiful, durable, and valuable than items made of synthetics.

Similarly, many modern individuals prefer homes built of natural materials, especially if they blend well with the environment. Thus, the popularity of sunbaked mud brick or adobe homes in the Southwest, locally quarried stone homes in the Texas hill country, and log homes in forested areas. Moreover, even if the building is not constructed of natural material, many modern homeowners insist the design of their home fits the region where it is built.

Outdoor living is also a part of most modern homes. Large patios, walls of windows, sun porches, and outdoor rooms all have roots in the Arts and Crafts movement, as does the idea of preserving the natural landscape that surrounds a home. In many ways, the Arts and Crafts movement, with its appreciation of nature and emphasis on the use of durable rather than disposable materials, fits well with the modern environmental movement.

According to the Colorado Arts and Crafts Society, "Because the style depends on simplicity and harmony among the home's many elements, and the lifestyle it advocates is holistic and planet-friendly, today it is even more relevant now than it was 100 years ago."[7] Indeed, when the Arts and Crafts movement began, its leaders had no idea that the philosophy would stand the test of time. Ideals like valuing fine craftsmanship, respecting the environment, living in harmony with nature, and surrounding oneself with simple, useful, beautiful things have proven timeless.

Social Reform Through Art

The Arts and Crafts movement was rooted in a philosophy that sought to reform society through art. It developed in Great Britain and then arrived in the United States, where it was reinterpreted to suit American life.

A Newly Industrialized Society

The Arts and Crafts movement began in Great Britain in the mid-nineteenth century as a reaction to the Industrial Revolution. Unlike other revolutions, the Industrial Revolution was not a violent uprising. It was called a revolution because it dramatically changed the nature of work and the way objects were made. It occurred as a result of the invention of machines like the steam engine and the power loom, which made it possible to mass-produce goods in factories.

Before the Industrial Revolution, craftspeople designed and handcrafted a product from conception to completion. This changed, however, with the Industrial Revolution when a work method known as division of labor increased efficiency. Division of labor involved dividing the creation of an object among many different workers, each of whom performed one small task and then passed the item onto the next worker until the product was complete. Rather than one person lovingly crafting a rug or a candlestick from start to finish, many workers and machines were involved in the making of each object. Division of labor made it possible to make more products faster and cheaper than ever before.

Factories employed lots of people, but working conditions were poor. Workers were not encouraged to take pride in their work, nor did they have the pleasure of actually creating something. Quantity was valued over quality, and little thought was given to a product's function, beauty, or durability. Profit was the driving force.

The factory system changed Great Britain's landscape as well. Factories polluted the air and waterways, and cities became overcrowded with factory workers. By the late 1800s, the simple lifestyle of the past had almost disappeared.

Medieval Roots

John Ruskin (1819–1900), a writer, art critic, and Oxford College professor, had no use for the Industrial Revolution and the cheap mass-produced objects manufactured by factories. He considered those items lacking in artistic value. He thought

In Great Britain in the 1800s, cheaper factory-made goods were slowly replacing high quality, hand-made ones.

Augustus Welby Northmore Pugin

*A*rchitect and designer A.W.N. Pugin (1812–1852) greatly influenced John Ruskin and William Morris. Pugin revered the Middle Ages. He believed that during the Middle Ages, people expressed the finest aspects of their character, including their religious faith, through the creative arts. He especially admired medieval Gothic architecture and design and the principle that the design of the interior and exterior of a building should harmonize. As a young man, he created a series of drawings providing details of medieval Gothic architecture and decoration. Pugin's drawings were so popular that at only nineteen years old, he was hired to design furniture for Windsor Castle. His drawings and regard for medieval craftsmanship inspired other architects and designers and helped create a revival of Gothic architecture and design in Great Britain.

Pugin designed many cathedrals and public buildings in Great Britain and was instrumental in the design of the Palace of Westminster in London. Pugin designed every aspect of the interiors and created drawings of all the exterior details.

that true art and beauty could be found in handcrafted objects made of natural materials and inspired by nature. Craftspeople, he felt, used not only their hands but also their hearts to create their work, while the factory system stifled creativity and denied workers the pleasure of designing and making an object with their own hands. Ruskin insisted that work should be creative and joyful, stimulating an individual's heart and mind. Work that gave individuals pleasure, he believed, made them better people. As he explains: "We are not sent into this world to do anything into which we cannot put our hearts . . . and what is not worth this effort is not to be done at all."[8] Ruskin's views that work should be pleasurable and handcrafted objects were art became guiding principles of the Arts and Crafts movement.

Ruskin wanted to reform society through art. He idealized Britain's pre-industrial past and looked back to the Middle Ages for inspiration, a period in history in which craftspeople were held in high esteem. Their work, Ruskin believed, gave them satisfaction and uplifted society with its beauty. Ruskin called for an end to the factory system and urged his supporters to refrain from buying mass-produced objects. His goal was to return Great Britain to a simpler, medieval lifestyle in which craftspeople took pleasure in their work, and art and beauty were a part of everyone's life.

Starting a Movement

Ruskin's ideas greatly impressed William Morris (1834–1896), and the two would become known as the founding fathers of the Arts and Crafts movement. Morris was a student at Oxford at the time Ruskin was trying to reform society. He studied architecture and art. Like Ruskin, he admired medieval life and craftsmanship, and he scorned mass-produced items and the Industrial Revolution that created these objects. Also, like Ruskin, Morris believed that people should derive pleasure from their work. After attending Ruskin's lectures, Morris vowed to make the reformation of society through art his life's work. "Apart from my desire to produce beautiful things," he wrote, "the leading passion of my life is hatred of modern civilization."[9]

Morris praised simple handcrafted objects as the highest form of art. He says: "Time was when the mystery and wonder of handicrafts were well acknowledged by the world, when imagination and fancy mingled with all things made by man; and in those days all handicraftsmen were artists, as we should now call them."[10] He also praised medieval Gothic style architecture with its pointed arches, verticality, many windows, and finely-crafted stone work, and the interdisciplinary approach medieval architects followed. Medieval architects not only designed buildings, they also cut stone, laid brick, sawed wood, painted walls, landscaped gardens, and decorated the building's interior. Morris believed this approach brought design unity to the various parts of a building.

The Poetic Red House

Putting his interdisciplinary philosophy into action, Morris commissioned his friend architect Philip Webb (1831–1915) in 1859 to collaborate with him on the design of a house in Bexleyheath, England. Webb would later become one of the most important British architects and designers of his time. Morris wanted the house to reflect his ideals and celebrate fine

The Gothic-inspired Red House is one of the first examples of the Arts and Crafts movement.

craftsmanship. The house, which is known as Red House, is one of the earliest and best known buildings of the Arts and Crafts movement. Ann Allen, author of the William Morris and Red House website, writes:

> Philip Webb the architect, and William Morris—his client and friend—were both at the beginning of their careers when the house was built in 1859 and 1860. It proved a focus for their ideas about architecture and art, for their love of the English and the medieval, and for their wish to do new things. It was to be a platform for their futures and those of their immediate circle, and also for many of the artistic developments of the late-19th century.[11]

Red House was designed in the Gothic style favored by Webb and Morris. Compared to the more popular Victorian style architecture of the day, characterized by lots of ornamentation, it was a simple, functional building. Morris insisted on using natural materials in its construction. Red House was constructed of red brick with a steep red-tiled roof and many windows. Morris believed that the house should be integrated with its surroundings and that the outside world should be a part of the home. With this in mind, he designed the gardens as a series of outdoor rooms that blended with the landscape and dressed up the plain building. According to art historian Wendy Hitchmough, "[The] house and its garden were inseparable ideologically, as a fusion of art and nature."[12]

On the north side of the house, Morris designed a large square formal garden surrounded by a trained hedge. He subdivided this garden into four smaller gardens, each of which was enclosed by a rose-covered fence. Morris's idea for these gardens within a garden was derived from medieval landscaping. Many art historians consider the gardens at Red House to have inspired an increased interest in gardening, associated with the Arts and Crafts movement in Great Britain. Morris's idea of integrating the outside world and the house itself became a guiding principle in Arts and Crafts architectural design.

Morris's philosophy of design unity was evident in the interior of Red House as well. He insisted each room and its furnishings harmonize with the next, and each piece be finely crafted. With the help of Webb and artists Edward Burne-Jones and Dante Gabriel Rossetti, among others, Morris designed and handcrafted the furniture, candlesticks, stained glass windows, murals, wallpaper, and embroidered wall hangings. Many of the embroidered wall hangings depicted designs of flowers, trees, and birds that mimicked the exterior landscape. The total effect, according to Rossetti, "[was] more a poem than a house."[13]

Morris and Company

The collaborative work involved in the creation of Red House led Morris to found a design company in 1861 with artists/designers Rossetti, Burne-Jones, Webb, Ford Madox Brown, P.P. Marshall, and bookkeeper Charles Faulkner. The company was originally named Morris, Marshall, Faulkner and Co., but was informally known as The Firm. In 1875, the name was changed to Morris and Co.

The Firm designed and made furniture, woven hangings, painted tiles, hand-knotted rugs, stained glass, murals, and wallpaper. Morris was especially involved in designing the patterns for the textiles and wallpaper. His designs were inspired by nature and his gardens at Red House. He used vegetable dyes rather than chemicals and printed the designs by hand. The company was also well known for its furniture and its stained glass designs, many of which are still found in churches throughout Great Britain.

Morris insisted that everything the company produced be handcrafted from natural materials. His initial goal was to produce finely crafted items cheaply, so that even the poorest consumer could own fine art. He states: "It is believed that good decoration, involving rather the luxury of taste than the luxury of costliness, will be found to be much less expensive than is generally supposed."[14] Unfortunately, the labor-intensive products the company created could not be made cheaply. Only the

William Morris designed wallpaper patterns, such as the sample pictured, by using his gardens as inspiration.

wealthy could afford Morris's products. Disillusioned, Morris eventually retired from the business, but his ideas and designs lived on.

Arts and Crafters Unite

Morris modeled his company after a medieval craft guild. Medieval craft guilds were organizations in which groups of craftsmen employed in the same occupation joined together to control the practice of their craft in their town. Craft guilds helped members when they were sick and established rules of the craft, quality standards, and fixed prices.

Morris liked the concept of a medieval craft guild. However, rather than limiting his organization to one particular craft, he

THE PRE-RAPHAELITES

*A*mong William Morris's circle of friends were a number of artists and writers known as the Pre-Raphaelites. They were a group of artists who banded together and rebelled against the accepted style of painting admired by the British art establishment at the time. This was the classical style of Italian Renaissance painter, Raphael (1483–1520), which was characterized by classical poses, elegant compositions, and an idealized view of the world. In 1848, the Pre-Raphaelites formed a secret society known as the Pre-Raphaelite Brotherhood through which they hoped to change the course of British painting. They favored realistic, detailed, and truthful artwork and insisted that artists must study nature before attempting to depict it.

Initially, the Pre-Raphaelite Brotherhood consisted of five artists: William Holman Hunt (1827–1910), Dante Gabriel Rossetti (1828–1882), John Everett Millais (1829–1896), Thomas Woolner (1825–1892), James Collinson (1825–1881), and writers William Michael Rossetti (1829–1919) and Frederic George Stephens (1828–1907). John Ruskin acted as a mentor to the group. He promoted the idea that artists should be true to nature. Of the group, Hunt, Rossetti, and Millais were most successful.

opened it up to artists practicing any craft connected with home design and construction. This model, he believed, would promote design unity while bringing artists together so that they could learn from each other. It was not long before other groups set up similar organizations. Members often belonged to more than one group. Most of these groups were interdisciplinary like Morris and Company, but some focused on one craft like their medieval predecessors. In keeping with the ideal of reforming society through art, some of these groups were charitable organizations that tried to help the poor by teaching them a craft.

One of the goals shared by these groups was to raise public awareness about the value and beauty of handicrafts. The Art Workers' Guild, which was founded in 1884, was among the most prominent group of the time. Members included Morris, Burne-Jones, metalsmith William Arthurs Smith Benson, artist and designer Walter Crane, architect J.D. Sedding, and artist T.J. Cobden-Sanderson, among others. The group met frequently to discuss art, design, and the reformation of society through art. The members embraced Morris's concept of collaboration between artists, architects, and craftspeople to achieve design unity. Indeed, the Guild's motto was "Art Is Unity."[15] They also supported the emerging principles of the Arts and Crafts movement popularized by Ruskin and Morris.

In 1888, the Guild gave rise to the Arts and Crafts Exhibition Society, which organized a joint exhibition of artists' and craftspeople's work in London. This was the first time the term *arts and crafts* was used to describe the growing movement. The members decided to organize and finance an exhibition because, at the time, the British art establishment routinely rejected architectural drawings and handicrafts from national art exhibitions, deeming such works inferior to paintings and sculpture. Followers of the Arts and Crafts movement believed that all forms of art had equal value. J.D. Sedding says, "All good art is one; all good artists are of one family."[16]

The exhibit, which featured architectural drawings, ceramics, metalwork, furniture, weavings, rugs, embroidery, sculptures, and paintings, was considered a radical display at the time. It was the first time fine art and handicrafts were displayed together at a large exhibition. The exhibition was a success financially and philosophically. It raised public interest in handcrafted objects and the principles of the Arts and Crafts movement. The Arts and Crafts Exhibition Society continued to hold exhibits periodically until the start of World War I in 1914.

The Movement Crosses the Atlantic

Ruskin and Morris's writings reached the United States even before the 1888 exhibit, as had objects crafted by Morris and Company that were being marketed in Boston, Massachusetts, and Chicago, Illinois, department stores. A number of U.S. architects and designers attended the exhibit. In turn, leaders of the British Arts and Crafts movement visited the United States, where they gave lectures and influenced U.S. architects and designers, including Frank Lloyd Wright and Charles Greene. By the turn of the century, many U.S. architects, designers, and craftspeople aligned themselves with the movement, and Arts and Crafts societies sprung up throughout the United States.

At first, the Arts and Crafts movement in the United States was strongly influenced by the principles of the British Arts and Crafts movement. However, it was not long before the movement was adapted to suit American culture. For instance, supporters of the American Arts and Crafts movement embraced the principles of finding joy in creating things and the importance

An oak desk by Gustav Stickley illustrates the simpler, more modern feel of the American Arts and Crafts style.

VICTORIAN STYLE

Before the simple style popularized by the Arts and Crafts movement became popular, many homes in Great Britain and the United States were decorated in Victorian style. Named after Great Britain's Queen Victoria, who ruled from 1837 to 1901, Victorian style was characterized by its lavishness. A typical Victorian home was brimming with richly carved, dark, formal looking furniture; ornate chandeliers; tasseled, beaded, and fringed lampshades and upholstery; multiple patterned, heavily textured wallpaper and elaborately framed pictures and animal trophy heads; window coverings in heavy rich fabrics like velvet or silk and masses of knick knacks, travel souvenirs, framed photos, vases, and other decorative objects on every available surface.

The style, which has often been described as cluttered and excessive, was one way that rich people could display their wealth. Mass production allowed middle class people to mimic the style and present the pretense of wealth.

of fine craftsmanship and unity of design. Unlike their British counterparts, who were pessimistic about the direction society was taking and wanted to return to a simpler time, Americans were proud of their country and optimistic about the future. Rather than taking inspiration from medieval art, they wanted to develop a style that reflected American life. They did this by using natural local materials in simple, yet innovative, designs.

Americans were also more accepting of the Industrial Revolution and the use of machines. Most U.S. Arts and Crafts advocates supported the use of machines to help make the work of craftspeople easier. As one of the leaders of the American Arts and Crafts movement, designer Gustav Stickley details: "Given the real need for production and the fundamental desire for self-expression, the machine can be put to all its legitimate uses as an aid to and preparation for, the work of the hand, and the result can be quite as vital and satisfying as the best work hand done."[17] In fact, as the movement progressed in the United States, the most successful craftspeople were those who combined the work of machines and handcraftsmanship.

Using machines in conjunction with handcraftsmanship made it possible to produce fine quality objects at a reasonable cost. As a result, more people could afford these products, which created more interest and demand for quality handicrafts and helped popularize the movement. A number of magazines dedicated to Arts and Crafts ideals also promoted the movement and the artists and craftspeople behind it. Stickley published a magazine titled *The Craftsman*. This publication and other magazines such as the *Ladies' Home Journal*, *House Beautiful*, and *House and Garden*, provided ideas for architects and craftspeople and served as authorities on home design and decor for U.S. consumers. Indeed, the publishers of *House Beautiful* describe the magazine as: "[The] only magazine in America devoted to simplicity, economy, and appropriateness in the home."[18]

The movement also received a big boost in 1901 at the Pan-American Exposition in Buffalo, New York. This was the first major exhibit in the United States devoted to the American Arts and Crafts movement. Featured items included stained glass designs by Louis Comfort Tiffany, furniture by Gustav Stickley, and ceramic pieces by various American potters and tile makers. In contrast to the work of British Arts and Crafts designers, the work exhibited in Buffalo borrowed less from medieval design. It was simpler, plainer, and had a more modern feel, which made it uniquely American. The exhibit was extremely popular with the public, and annual exhibits were held at the Chicago Art Institute from 1902 to 1921.

Settlement Houses and Utopian Communities

The British idea of using art to help improve society caught on with many Americans, especially as a way to help immigrants adjust to life in America and make life more enjoyable for housewives and laborers. The notion that art could influence quality of life was evident in 1889 when two wealthy women, Jane Addams and Ellen Gates Starr, founded Hull House in Chicago. It was a settlement house, an institution established in an inner-city that provides educational and social services to people in the surrounding neighborhood. Craftspeople, artists, scholars, and architects such as Wright volunteered at Hull House, where they offered classes in crafts such as woodworking, silversmithing, china painting, and ceramics. These classes

An instructor at Hull House demonstrates the art of weaving to two women.

had multiple purposes. They spread the principles of the Arts and Crafts movement while providing marketable skills to the many immigrants who lived in the neighborhood. The classes also helped popularize handicrafts as hobbies. The idea that people could achieve personal fulfillment in their free time through their hobbies was an important aspect of the Arts and Crafts movement. Indeed, popular magazines of the time commonly published different hobby projects.

Hull House was so successful that it became a model for other settlement houses. The popularity of craft classes also led to public high schools offering students training in crafts like woodworking, metalworking, embroidery, design, and sewing. These classes were categorized as manual training or industrial arts. Even institutions of higher learning, such as the Pratt Institute in Brooklyn, New York, and Alfred University in Alfred, New York, began offering degrees in design and ceramics.

Other reformers besides Jane Addams and Ellen Gates Starr started utopian communities populated by craftspeople. The most famous was the Roycroft community founded by Elbert Hubbard (1815–1915) in 1895. The community in East Aurora, New York, was a place where craftspeople lived and worked together. Hubbard, a writer, artist, salesman, and philosopher, was a loyal follower of the Arts and Crafts movement and the teachings of Ruskin and Morris.

The Roycrofters, as they were known, created ceramics, glass objects, metal work, furniture, and leather goods. They also published beautifully illustrated books and periodicals written by Hubbard and printed on handmade paper. Hubbard promoted the Arts and Crafts movement and the Roycrofters' products in his writing. The Roycrofters built shops in the community where they sold their wares. They also built communal homes in which multiple families lived together; a school and playground for their children; a farm; a bank; and a hotel for the many tourists and art collectors that visited the community. The community began with 175 residents and swelled to more than five hundred by 1910. Hubbard encouraged the residents

In the early 1900s the Roycroft community in East Aurora, New York, helped grow the Arts and Crafts movement by creating handcrafted furniture, ceramics, and other wares.

to learn from each other and become skilled at multiple crafts, so their work would never become tedious. As he explains: "When a pressman or a typesetter found his work monotonous . . . he felt at liberty to leave it and turn stonemason or carpenter."[19] The community operated until 1938. Today, fourteen of the buildings, including a museum, are open to the public, and items produced by the Roycrofters are much valued.

By the beginning of the twentieth century, the Arts and Crafts movement was flourishing in the United States. It encompassed everything from architecture, home furnishing, decorative objects, and textiles to printing. The philosophy and ideals changed to better suit Americans' optimistic view of the world as the movement crossed the Atlantic. These changes helped make art available to everyone.

"Buildings, Too, Are Children of the Earth"

Up until the latter part of the 1800s, most architecture in the United States was modeled after European styles. The result was a jumble of various styles taken from various countries and time periods that did not reflect local environment or culture. Often a hodgepodge of architectural features and building materials were thrown together on one building. Nor was the purpose of a building considered in its design. Supporters of the Arts and Crafts movement preferred simpler, more natural architecture designed to reflect the setting, the building's function, and American life. As Frank Lloyd Wright asserts: "A fire house should not resemble a French Chateau, a bank a Greek temple and a university a Gothic cathedral. . . . Every great architect is—necessarily—a great poet. He must be a great original interpreter of his time, his day, his age."[20]

During the late nineteenth and early twentieth century, U.S. architects created a variety of innovative, uniquely American buildings in harmony with the surrounding landscape. Designs reflected the distinct regional differences of the geographically diverse nation. Consequently, there was no one architectural style that defined the American Arts and Crafts movement. As writer Charles Keeler explains in his 1906 book, *The Simple Home*:

> It has often been pointed out that all sound art is an expression springing from the nature which environs it. . . . A home, for example, must be adapted to the climate, the landscape, and the life in which it is to serve its part. In New England we must have New England homes; in Alabama, Alabama homes, and in California, California homes. We cannot import the one bodily into the other surroundings without introducing jarring notes.[21]

Despite regional differences, buildings associated with the American Arts and Crafts movement shared a number of common elements: They were in tune with the local environment and climate, made of local materials, designed to integrate the indoors and outdoors, and simple and well crafted. The finest designs looked almost as if they were part of the landscape and were known as genuine or organic architecture; or, as Wright put it: "Buildings, too, are the children of the earth and sun."[22]

The interiors took advantage of natural light. Rooms were bright and airy and opened onto each other. It was often possible to see through an Arts and Crafts house from front to back. Design and trim were simple but carefully crafted. The simplicity and the use of local materials helped to make Arts and Crafts structures affordable to more people, as did the use of machines to help prepare raw materials. For the first time in U.S. history, ordinary people could afford beautifully crafted homes.

Form Follows Function

The Arts and Crafts movement inspired many talented architects who practiced organic architecture. Perhaps the most uniquely American buildings originated in the Midwest. There, an architect named Louis Sullivan (1856–1924) sought to develop an

The historic Prudential Guaranty Building in Buffalo, New York, designed by Louis Sullivan in 1894, was one of the first steel-supported high-rise buildings.

original architectural style free of historical imitation—a style that reflected American life. He is considered by many art historians to be the father of modern American architecture. Sullivan studied architecture for one year at the Massachusetts Institute of Technology before beginning work as an architect. In 1873, he moved to Chicago where a building boom was taking place in the wake of the Great Chicago Fire of 1871. His first job there involved erecting one of the earliest steel-framed multi-storied buildings in the United States. Before then, buildings had to be supported solely by the weight of their walls, which limited their height. The development of steel made it possible to build high-rise buildings. Sullivan embraced the idea of building skyward and the opportunity to develop a new style of architecture, which accentuated a building's function, geometric shape, and simplicity.

Sullivan was also concerned with linking the design and function of his buildings. He insisted that the outside of his building harmonize with the interior structure and the building's specific purpose. It was Sullivan who coined the phrase, "form follows function," which means a building's purpose should be the starting point for its design. For example, in his design of Chicago's Auditorium Theatre, a concert hall completed in 1889, Sullivan designed the theater in the shape of a hollow cone so that sound would be equally clear throughout the building.

Sullivan designed many public buildings, including Chicago's Stock Exchange Building. He also designed houses. His philosophy that form follows function became a guiding principle for twentieth-century architectural design.

Frank Lloyd Wright's Prairie School

Sullivan influenced more than architectural designs. He also mentored a young architect named Frank Lloyd Wright (1867–1959). Wright had had no formal training as an architect when Sullivan hired him as his assistant in 1888. Wright worked for Sullivan for five years. During this time, he learned all he could about architecture. In 1893, Wright established his own architectural practice. Inspired by the Arts and Crafts movement and Sullivan's philosophy of organic, functional architecture, Wright's work embodied the essence of the Midwest. Wright's

THE SPIRIT OF ART

Followers of the American Arts and Crafts movement insisted that art in all its forms should reflect American life and culture. In an article in the January 1906 issue of The Craftsman, *American poet and novelist Edwin Wiley expands on this belief:*

> Nothing so reveals the true life of a people or an epoch as its art. Neither history nor religion offers such a sure test of the heights to which the spirit of an age has risen. View it as you will, art is molded by the forces that environ it, revealing on one hand the art and soul of its creator, and on the other the heart and soul of his age. However much an artist may think himself detached from his surroundings, however passionately he may turn to other ages for inspiration—nay, even though he feels himself gifted with prophetic prescience [the ability to predict the future], and can project himself to ages unborn—still he can no more throw aside the mantle of his environment than he can escape the intangible, viewless air that gives him breath and life.

Edwin Wiley. "The Spirit of Art." *The Craftsman*, January 1906, p. 529.

style became known as the Prairie School of Architecture and influenced many other architects.

Wright mainly designed residential buildings ranging from small houses for typical U.S. families to large mansions. His designs were characterized by simplicity, use of natural materials, and color schemes that mirrored the surrounding prairie

wheat fields: long horizontal lines, gently sloped roofs with overhanging eaves or edges, rows of windows, wide porches, and careful placement on the site.

These elements tied Wright's creations to the landscape in a way that made the buildings appear to be part of the natural environment. As he details:

> We of the Middle West are living on the prairie. The prairie has a beauty of its own and we should recognize and accentuate this natural beauty, its quiet level. Hence, gently sloping roofs, low proportions, quiet sky lines, suppressed heavy-set chimneys, and sheltering overhangs, low terraces and out-reaching walls sequestering private gardens.[23]

Wright's genius in integrating a building with its natural surroundings can best be seen in Fallingwater, a multi-level house he designed in 1935 that is situated over a waterfall in southwestern Pennsylvania. According to an article on the Fallingwater website, "It's a house that doesn't even appear to stand on solid ground, but instead stretches out over a 30' waterfall."[24]

Fallingwater is constructed of sandstone quarried on site. The stones separate concrete tiers that form the different levels of the building and are suspended over the waterfall. Mature trees grow through the building, and a huge boulder is part of the living room. The house, which is now open to the public as a National Historic Landmark, appeared on the cover of *Time* magazine in 1938.

The interiors of Wright's buildings were also innovative. In the past, the interiors of most U.S. houses were boxlike, consisting of many small, dark rooms. Wright rejected this design. He added rows of art glass windows and opened up interior space, creating bright, functional rooms that overlapped and flowed into each other and gave the illusion of spaciousness. In many instances, he used walls to define areas rather than to enclose them. Subtle changes in ceiling height also helped define rather than enclose living areas. To further simplify the home and

Opposite page: Frank Lloyd Wright's Fallingwater, designed in 1935, is an example of how Wright integrated a building with its natural surroundings.

BERNARD MAYBECK

Bernard Maybeck (1862–1957) was an important architect and follower of the Arts and Crafts movement. Born in New York, New York, Maybeck studied architecture in Paris, France, at the prestigious École des Beaux-Arts. Upon returning to the United States, he moved to California, where he became the first professor of architecture at the University of California, Berkeley.

In 1903, he left the university and set up an architecture firm in San Francisco, California. He designed a total of about 150 homes, public buildings, and churches throughout the San Francisco Bay area, especially in the Berkeley Hills. His designs were inspired by the local landscape and climate, California missions, and Craftsman-style bungalows. They were characterized by integration with the surrounding landscape, use of native redwood, large windows, bright colors, and handcrafted details.

One of his most famous creations is San Francisco's Palace of Fine Arts, which he designed for the 1915 Panama-Pacific International Exposition as an art gallery in the style of an ancient ruin. Maybeck mentored many young architects during his life, including Julia Morgan who became one of the first licensed female architects in the United States.

ensure design unity, Wright used wood and stone on interior walls and included simple, functional, built-in cabinets, bookcases, and other furniture of his own design. The total effect was a work of art in which form, function, and beauty were flawlessly combined. He used machines to help in the construction of his designs; therefore, his designs were also affordable to more Americans.

Wright's designs owed much to his mentor, Sullivan, and to the Arts and Crafts movement. As authors Elizabeth Cumming and Wendy Kaplan write: "His belief in fidelity to the inherent nature of materials, unity of design, responding to the landscape and creating a democratic art were all touchstones of the movement."[25]

The Bungalow

Like Wright's designs, another form of architecture, the bungalow, also adhered to the principles of the Arts and Crafts movement. These buildings' simplicity, use of natural materials, suitability to the environment, and design that integrated the indoors and outdoors, made the bungalow the style of architecture most closely associated with the Arts and Crafts movement. The word bungalow comes from the Hindi word *bangla*, meaning a low, thatched house. Banglas were designed with ventilation and protection from the tropical sun in mind. British

The bungalow is one of the most commonly recognizable legacies of the Arts and Crafts movement.

colonizers in India adapted these buildings for their homes, calling them bungalows. British bungalows were characterized by large shaded verandas or porches and ample outdoor living space.

The concept was well suited to southern California's mild climate and outdoor lifestyle, where the American bungalow first developed. U.S. architects used the basic concept to design uniquely American style bungalows. American bungalows lacked the ornamentation of those built by the British. They were also more finely crafted. Typically, they were one, or one and a half stories in height with large windows and a broad, roofed, partially enclosed entry porch. The porch served as an outdoor room that connected the exterior and interior of the house. According to authors James C. Massey and Shirley Maxwell, it "was designed for comfort—shelter from the elements and a companionable spot to sit and chat and watch (or wave at) the passing world."[26]

The entry porch usually opened directly into the living room, which opened into the dining room. The bedrooms were in the back of the house, where there was usually a second porch that was used as a sleeping porch in warm weather. The sleeping porch was often screened, or it was enclosed with one wall open to the outdoors but shielded by canvas, which could be rolled up or down like the walls of a tent.

Everything about the bungalow was simple, functional, and well crafted. The interior and exterior walls were typically constructed of local wood, which was treated with a wood stain to bring out its natural color, providing design unity while blending the building with the natural world around it.

Craftsman Homes

At first, bungalows were used mainly as vacation homes. It was Gustav Stickley (1858–1942) who popularized them as year-round dwellings. Stickley was born in Wisconsin. Because his father died when he was a teenager, he assumed the responsibility of supporting his family. He worked as a stone mason

for a few years; then, he took a job in his uncle's furniture factory, which was his first experience working with furniture. He became quite interested in furniture design, forming a furniture design company with his brothers, Albert and Charles in 1883. The brothers did not work well together, and in 1898 Stickley formed his own furniture design company, the Gustav Stickley Company. He changed the name to the Craftsman Workshops in 1903. From then on, Stickley's designs were marketed under the brand name Craftsman.

Stickley was a firm supporter of the Arts and Crafts movement. In fact, many art historians credit Stickley as the person most responsible for popularizing Arts and Crafts principles and designs in the United States. Stickley's magazine, *The Craftsman*, promoted Arts and Crafts ideals and showcased his furniture designs. Each month it featured a different house plan with advice on decorating, landscaping, and furniture for the home. Stickley's aim was to provide his readers plans for a

Craftsman homes could be adapted to suit different family sizes. Pictured here is a large Foursquare home, which is equivalent to a two-story bungalow.

complete, unified home environment. His integrated designs, featuring extensive unadorned woodwork and furnishings constructed of quality natural materials, became a hallmark of the American Arts and Crafts movement. Although he had no formal training as an architect, most of the designs were original. By the time the magazine stopped publication in 1916, it had featured more than 222 house plans.

Stickley's architectural designs became known as Craftsman homes. All were based on the bungalow, which Stickley describes as: "beautiful because it is planned and built to meet simple needs in the simplest and most direct way."[27] Stickley designed his houses with middle class families in mind. His guiding design principle was:

> To substitute the luxury of taste for the luxury of costliness; to teach that beauty does not imply elaboration or ornament; to employ only those forms and materials which make for simplicity, individuality, and dignity of effect.[28]

Stickley adapted bungalow designs to suit different size families and different regions of the country. For instance, for the East Coast where there was less room to spread out, Stickley designed Foursquare homes, essentially two-story bungalows with four rooms on each floor.

Kit Homes

Stickley's Craftsman homes were so popular that other magazines also started publishing house plans. Some companies, including the catalog company Sears and Roebuck, even provided ready-to-assemble kit homes in the Craftsman style. Ready-to-assemble kit homes were essentially houses in a box. Customers selected a particular house design from a catalog. Easy-to-follow house plans and all the materials needed to build the house were then shipped to the customer. The homes were usually small and affordable, and they were known for their high quality.

The affordability of kit homes made them extremely popular and fit with the social consciousness of the Arts and Crafts movement. According to Nebraska architect J.M. Edgar:

> Kit houses were a giant step in affordable house building. Ready-cut houses were 'assembled' from lumber already cut to the correct size at the manufacturer's mill. Everything from nails to millwork, even paint was shipped . . . to the building site. Pre-cut lumber and trim, and pre-assembled doors, windows and mouldings, even cabinets were carefully numbered to match the plan books that guided assembly.[29]

"A Reason for Every Detail"

Whereas both Stickley's Craftsman homes and ready-to-assemble kit houses were designed with affordability in mind,

A look inside the Gamble House in Pasadena, California, reveals an abundance of beautiful wood and many special details, such as the inglenook pictured here.

two brothers, Charles Sumner Greene (1868–1957) and Henry Mather Greene (1870–1954) designed large, impressive bungalow style homes for wealthy people in California. Their designs, known as *ultimate bungalows*, are considered architectural masterpieces showcasing the very best of the American Arts and Crafts movement.

The Greene brothers were born in Ohio and grew up in St. Louis, Missouri, where they studied woodworking and metal work at a manual training school. It was there that they were introduced to the principles of the Arts and Crafts movement and developed their fascination with natural materials and fine craftsmanship. They briefly attended the Massachusetts Institute of Technology School of Architecture but did not graduate. In 1893, when their parents moved to Pasadena, California, the brothers joined them. The next year they set up their architectural firm Greene and Greene in Pasadena.

The Greenes' work was characterized by its simplicity. They took pride in showcasing the structural composition of a building. Exposed beams and brackets and visible rounded joinery were common elements in all their work. Fine craftsmanship, exemplified by hand crafted wood, copper, and iron work, was another important element of a Greene design. So was unity of design; harmony with nature; and, most famously, the brothers' almost obsessive attention to detail. As Henry Greene explained: "The whole construction was carefully thought out and there was a reason for every detail."[30]

With this in mind, the brothers not only designed buildings, they created complete environments, designing the gardens, walkways, built-in and moveable furniture, door knobs and cabinet pulls, art glass, rugs, tapestries, table linens, lamps, and household tools like candlesticks and fireplace screens. According to architect Morgan Yost, "They were able at that time to do a house for a wealthy family that would be complete right down to the last table cover and throw, all the furnishings. It was amazing to see such complete perfection."[31]

One of the Greenes' most famous buildings is the Gamble House in Pasadena. It is the best preserved of all the Greene

ARTS AND CRAFTS GARDENS

Before the Arts and Crafts era, most gardens were formal, symmetrical, and carefully planned. Many were filled with exotic plants. They did not reflect the surrounding landscape or the home itself.

The Arts and Crafts movement inspired people to view the garden as an extension of the local environment and the house. Two English artists, Gertrude Jekyll and William Robinson, pioneered a new type of garden design linked to the Arts and Crafts movement. Both promoted more natural gardens that featured profusions of native flowering plants such as roses, hollyhocks, and sunflowers, which were also featured in interior textile designs. They planted these in masses, rather than traditional straight lines. They also grouped plants by color and form to create unity of design.

American gardeners favored plants local to their surroundings. Thus, in California, plants like cacti, poppies, lilies, and wild grasses were incorporated into gardens. Prairie plants dominated Midwestern gardens, and different varieties of evergreens were common in Pacific Northwestern gardens.

The profession of landscape architecture, which developed about 1900, was an outgrowth of the interest in gardening associated with the Arts and Crafts movement.

brothers' work. In 1977, it was named a National Historic Landmark. The Greenes designed the house, garden, and furnishings for industrialist David Gamble in 1908. The huge three-story house had five bathrooms, three sleeping porches, two wide terraces, a large kitchen and butler's pantry, and a large top floor billiards room with windows on all four sides. The brothers left no detail to chance; they designed every peg, downspout, air vent, opening, light switch, and stained glass light fixture in the house. One of the most interesting features was the artistic use of multiple types of wood for wood paneling, furniture, stair posts, mantels, and cabinetry. Author Pamela Todd writes: "In March 1908 the *Pasadena Daily News* raved about the mahogany dining room, the teakwood living room, the oak used in the den and the white cedar elsewhere."[32]

Mission Style

The classic Mission style is exemplified in the Irving Gill-designed Oceanside (California) City Hall, built in 1934.

California was the original home for another style of architecture known as Mission style, which borrowed from the state's Spanish colonial past. Early Spanish missionaries built religious settlements known as missions. A mission consisted of simple

unadorned buildings made of adobe (sunbaked clay) with white walls, large inner courtyards, numerous patios, and arched entryways. The missions' stark simplicity, clean lines, sturdiness, economy in the use of materials, functionality, and compatibility with California's climate and landscape inspired architect Irving Gill (1870–1936) who adapted the style to suit his philosophy and designs.

Gill was born in Tully, New York. He had little formal education and no academic training in art or architecture. As a young man he moved to Chicago, where he worked as an assistant to Sullivan at the same time as Wright. In 1893, Gill moved to San Diego, California. Gill was highly influenced by Sullivan's philosophy of form and function. In an effort to optimize a building's functionality and beauty, he simplified architecture to its most basic geometric forms, removing all ornamentation. This included eliminating window sills, baseboards, wood paneling, fireplace mantels, ledges, or chair rails. According to Gill, such simplicity allowed the building's natural beauty to shine through, a philosophy that would later become known as minimalism. He explained: "If we omit everything useless from a structural point of view we will come to see the great beauty of the straight line, to see the charm that lies in perspective, the force in light and shadow, the power in balanced masses, the fascination of color that plays on a smooth wall."[33]

Following the social ideals of the Arts and Crafts movement, Gill was also concerned with providing beautiful, functional homes for everyone. He designed grand houses for wealthy people, middle-class homes, cottages on the Rancho Barona Indian Reservation, homes for poor Mexican farm workers, and an apartment complex for laborers consisting of simple cottages surrounded by gardens. Before he died, he was working on a design for housing for the unemployed. He also designed churches, schools, and public buildings. Most of his buildings were constructed of concrete, which imitated the sturdiness and plainness of adobe. Like the Spanish missions, his designs featured flat tiled roofs without eaves or overhangs, arched doorways, and courtyards and patios, which connected and united the indoors and outdoors. His rooms were cube-like in shape, and exterior and interior walls were painted white.

Gill's designs were quite different from those of the Greene brothers, just as the Greene brothers' designs could not be confused with those of Stickley or Wright. Yet the work of these architects had much in common. Following the principles of the Arts and Crafts movement, they designed new types of buildings that valued simplicity, beauty, and usefulness over ornamentation. Their designs were inspired by the United States' past, culture, and geography. Such buildings, characterized by open floor plans, multiple windows, porches, patios, courtyards, and verandas welcomed the outdoors in. They were modern, comfortable, affordable, and uniquely American.

Home, Hearth, and Family

*A*rts and crafts designers believed that living in a comfort-able home filled with simple, useful, finely-crafted objects had a positive impact on family life. As a result, architects were as concerned with the interior decor as they were with the build-ing itself. Their goal was to create a serene atmosphere in which each part of the home harmonized with the next, and in which families could thrive. Charles Keeler explains:

> Simplicity, significance, utility, harmony—these are the watchwords. . . . How often we enter an apartment, full of elegant and beautiful things, in which there is no continuity of idea, no central thought which dominates the place! And when we come upon some simple room about which there is a sense of rest and harmony, we do not always stop to analyze the effect to see how it is produced. We feel that there is an intangible idea [in] back of all the detail, and it pleases us.[34]

To ensure that the interior décor blended with the all-over design of the house, architects created furniture to fit the building. Flooring material, ceiling beams, fireplace surrounds, paneling, and moldings also provided continuity by creating a pattern of repeating geometric forms, directional lines, and colors throughout the house. Individual furniture designers, too, strove to create simple, good quality, well-crafted pieces that complemented the clean lines of Arts and Crafts homes. As Hugh M.G. Garden, an architect who worked with Frank Lloyd Wright, details: "All arts are alike in that the common end and aim of each is the weaving of a pattern. The pattern to be woven in the designing of a house is one of forms, lines, colors and textures; relating, repeating, and contrasting one with the other, creating rhythms, directions, accents."[35] The end result was a functional work of art designed to enhance family living.

The Heart and Soul of a House

The fireplace was one aspect of a home's design that Arts and Crafts designers believed played a central role in family life. In the past, the fireplace provided homes with heat, light, and a place to cook. Most Arts and Crafts-era homes had radiators, a furnace, a stove, and electricity, making a fireplace unnecessary. Nevertheless, almost all Arts and Crafts-era homes had at least one fireplace, and it was considered the heart and soul of the home. In an artistic sense, it served as a focal point that drew the eyes into the home. Functionally, it provided warmth and beauty and was a cozy spot for families to gather. As an article in *The Craftsman* declares: "As the heart is to the human body, so is the fireplace to the home. From it flows the sustaining power of family life."[36]

To physically define the fireplace as a family gathering place, many architects surrounded it with a seating alcove known as an *inglenook*. Inglenooks were oak benches with high backs topped by soft leather seat and back cushions. Typically, the ceiling over the inglenook was lower than the ceiling in the rest of the room, which added a feeling of snugness. Other furnishings such as a drop-front desk and bookcases with beautifully designed stained-glass doors were also commonly built around the fireplace. The whole effect was one of hominess, warmth, and beauty.

The fireplace was a work of art. The chimney was constructed of brick, concrete, or stone. Local fieldstone and river rocks were quite popular. Their rustic look blended well with the exterior landscape. The hearth, which included the floor of the fireplace and the outside surround, was faced with a number of materials such as brick, tile, stone, or metal.

Brick was especially popular. Bricks might be red, gold, or tan, colors that blended well with exterior landscapes. They were made from clay, a natural substance, and they were economical, particularly *clinker bricks*. Clinker bricks were misshapen, glassy bricks that were usually discarded. Their irregular shape,

Most Arts and Crafts houses have at least one fireplace, which acts as the centerpiece of the home and a natural gathering spot.

ARTS AND CRAFTS-ERA RUGS

Arts and Crafts-era houses usually had wood floors, which were often partially covered with area rugs. An article in Arts and Crafts *magazine examines these rugs:*

Traditional American, machine-made carpets were . . . popular. . . . Often quite simple in design, a solid field with a patterned border, these were frequently used in several contiguous rooms to tie spaces together. Border patterns were often based on nature: pine trees and acorns, thistles, ginkgo leaves.

Not all carpets were elaborate, or expensive. Simple grass mats from China or Japan were advised in *The Craftsman* and other magazines as appropriate complements for the natural woodwork and "honesty" of the Arts and Crafts home. Rag rugs also gained favor. . . .

Native American crafts were the country's only true handicrafts, according to Gustav Stickley. The strong, geometric designs in American Indian blankets and rugs enhanced the straight angular lines of his furniture, Stickley suggested. Thus many Craftsman homes of the period proudly hung a Navajo blanket on the wall above a leather-covered settle, or placed a geometrically patterned Native American runner beneath the Morris chair in the fireplace inglenook.

Patricia Poore. "Carpet History in the Arts and Crafts Home." *Arts and Crafts Homes and the Revival,* October 31, 2012. http://artsandcraftshomes.com/carpet-history-in-the-ac-home.

interesting texture, and low cost made them popular with followers of the Arts and Crafts movement.

Laying the bricks was an art. The best work was accomplished by masons who created interesting patterns by laying bricks in multiple ways called *bonds*. According to author Jane Powell, "Flemish bond features one brick turned on end every other brick. Multicolored brick patterns were referred to as tapestry brick. Brick also could be laid unevenly and randomly, known as eccentric brickwork."[37]

Batchelder Plays with Tile

Artistry was also on display in tile work. Many hearths and fireplace mantels were faced with tile. Often plain tiles were combined with art tiles, the term used for decorated tiles. Art tiles were also used on staircase risers, the vertical part of a stair that connects one stair to the next, and on garden fountains. Some of the most beautifully designed tiles of the period were created by Ernest Batchelder (1875–1957).

Batchelder was a teacher, designer, writer, and ceramicist. Before starting the Batchelder Tile Company in Pasadena, California, in 1909, he studied design in England and taught art and design at Harvard University and the Throop Polytechnic Institute in Pasadena. Batchelder's career as a tile maker began modestly when he built a kiln in his backyard and began experimenting with the craft. His experiments eventually grew into a business that employed more than one hundred craftspeople.

Making beautiful tiles takes skill. It involves molding clay into thin pieces either by placing the clay in a special frame by hand or machine. Next, designs are carved onto the clay. Then, the tiles are coated with a glaze that imparts color. Or, they may be left unglazed, in which case they retain the natural color of the clay. Clay colors range from sand to a reddish brown. Finally, the tiles are baked or fired in a kiln, a special oven that can reach up to 2000°F (1093°C). Some tiles are decorated with hand painted designs, which are painted after the tiles cool.

Batchelder molded each tile by hand. Before firing the tiles, he left them out in his backyard to dry, where "cats and chickens frequently walked over them offering a pleasing variation of texture."[38] Batchelder prided himself on the uniqueness of his tiles. Even when his business expanded and machines were used

Ernest Batchelder tiles are found in many Arts and Crafts–style homes built in the early 1900s.

to help the craftspeople, Batchelder insisted that no two tiles created by his company were exactly the same.

Batchelder's tiles were known for their subdued colors, typically brown with a blue glaze rubbed into the indentations in the designs. His designs included geometric shapes, Viking-style ships, and animals. Peacocks, in particular, were a favorite of Batchelder. He was also known for his depictions of trees and flowers local to California. His work was so popular that nearly every home built in Pasadena between 1910 and 1928 contained Batchelder's tiles.

The Warmth of Wood

Wood also figured prominently in Arts and Crafts-era homes. It added a feeling of warmth and friendliness. It also provided a unifying element that turned a house from a series of rooms to a finely designed whole. Wood floors connected one room to the next; wood paneling covered interior walls either from floor to ceiling or as wainscoting that lined the lower half of the walls; wood moldings (strips of wood used to cover junctions between walls and floors, windows, doors, or ceilings) framed windows and doors and served as baseboards; and sturdy wood beams ran across the ceilings. Gustav Stickley, who was known for his Craftsman home designs, is also admired for the way he incorporated wood into various architectural elements. In her biography of Stickley, author Mary Ann Smith describes how he used wood to unify the different elements in his own house:

> First, the horizontal [wood] band running at the tops of the doors and windows connects all the walls on the ground floor. Below this band, the walls are paneled with vertical boards, above they are plastered. Then, the squared rectangular [ceiling] beams that run the length of the house, from the living room to the library, emphasize the perspective openness of the interior space. As the floor of broad chestnut boards spreads continuously through the downstairs space, the only division between the rooms becomes the cross beams that serve as a visual separation.[39]

Because of the way it harmonized with the environment, local wood was commonly used. Oak, in particular, was a top choice. It was rarely painted. Instead it was rubbed with wax to preserve its natural color and texture, or it was lightly stained. Stickley developed a process in which he exposed wood to fumes emitted by ammonia, which darkened and enriched the wood without obscuring the wood's natural grain. The ripple of the grain, and the way it created different tones and textures on the wood were hallmarks of Arts and Crafts design. As Stickley details:

> Woodwork should be so finished that its inherent [natural] color quality is deepened and mellowed as if by time and its surface made pleasantly smooth

without sacrificing the woody quality that comes from frankly revealing its natural texture. When this is done, the little sparkling irregularity of the grain allows a play of light over the surface that seems to give it almost a soft radiance.[40]

Wood was also on display in built-in furnishings. By helping to unify the different elements of the home, creating built-in furniture provided the architect more control of his artistic vision. "I tried to make my clients see that furniture and furnishing . . . should be seen as minor parts of the building itself,"[41] Frank Lloyd Wright explains. Built-ins included china cabinets known as sideboards, bookshelves, fireplace seats, and window seats that provided a comfortable place to admire the outside world. Some homes also had built-in breakfast nooks consisting of wooden benches and a table built into a corner of the kitchen as well as built-in wardrobes in the bedrooms with drawers and a rod for hanging clothes. The design of built-in furniture varied, but simplicity, fine craftsmanship, and utility were common to all designs.

Stickley Has a Mission

Simple, lovingly crafted, moveable wood furniture was another key component of Arts and Crafts design. Stickley, who designed furniture as well as homes, was among the most famous and influential of the movement's furniture designers. His designs were characterized by their straight lines, proportions, simplicity, utility, careful craftsmanship, and use of natural materials.

Known as both Craftsman and Mission style furniture, Stickley's designs got the latter name partly because of their simple style reminiscent of seats in California's Spanish missions, and partly because of the designer's insistence that his furniture had a mission to accomplish. "That mission," a magazine article of the time states, "is to teach that the first laws of furniture making should be good material, true proportion, and honest workmanship."[42]

CANDACE WHEELER

Candace Wheeler (1827–1923) was an interior, glass, and textile designer. She is often called the "Mother of American Interior Design." When Wheeler was a child, her mother taught her how to weave and embroider. She studied painting in school, married young, and was the mother of four children.

Wheeler is best known for helping to open the field of interior design to women. After the Civil War, many war widows needed a way to earn a living. Wheeler founded the Society of Decorative Art in New York City in 1877, which was dedicated to the sale of paintings, woodcarvings, pottery, tapestries, and decorative needlework crafted by women. Besides running the business and creating her own tapestries and art glass, Wheeler offered courses in design for women. In addition, she designed the interior of the Woman's Building at the World's Fair in Chicago in 1893. Toward the end of her life, she promoted rug making as a business for rural women, became a popular writer of fiction, and designed her own home.

Stickley's work was inspired by the work of British Arts and Crafts designers such as William Morris and American Shaker-style furniture. The Shakers were a religious sect known for their handicrafts, especially their finely crafted, simple, durable furniture. The Shakers insisted that everything they made must be honest in construction and appearance. To them, painting furniture or adding ornamentation was considered dishonest and contrary to their religious beliefs.

Stickley, too, believed in honest construction. Stickley's designs were simple straight-lined oak pieces that lacked

A Gustav Stickley double-door book-case is constructed in the Craftsman, or Mission, style known for its simplicity and utility.

carvings and other adornment. Instead of decoration, he emphasized shape, proportions, and structural quality. The last included exposing features of construction like the wood join-ery and highlighting the wood's grain. For pieces that required hinges and pulls, he designed rustic looking hardware out of iron, brass, and hammered copper that harmonized with the overall design of the furniture.

Stickley also believed that honestly constructed furniture should be comfortable, durable, and useful. He rejected exaggerated designs that were more concerned with appearance than with utility. With that goal in mind, he upholstered his chairs with comfortable natural materials such as leather in subdued colors that blended with the landscape and helped create a serene atmosphere.

Stickley's simple, well-crafted, functional designs became symbols of the Arts and Crafts movement. Because he used machines to construct the basic components of his pieces, which were then handed over to skilled craftsmen for assembling and finishing, they were affordable. This added to their popularity. In fact, Stickley's designs were so popular that a number of other companies began producing similar pieces, including two rival companies owned by Stickley's brothers.

The Father of Reclining Chairs

Stickley designed many types of furniture. Morris chairs, which Stickley adapted from chairs designed by the William Morris Company, are among the most well-known of his designs. Morris chairs were the earliest recliners. They had a moveable back that could be set at four or five different angles. The first Morris chairs were designed by the William Morris Company in Britain and were delicate and formal. Stickley adapted the design to suit American tastes. His chairs were larger, sturdier, plainer, and more comfortable than the British version. Stickley advertised his design as: "a big deep chair that means comfort to a tired man when he comes home after the day's work."[43]

Stickley designed several versions of the Morris chair. The chairs usually had straight or bowed arms, and a slatted back. The back was attached to the seat with hinges and supported from behind by a rod. In order to change the reclining angle, the user had to walk to the back of the chair and adjust the rod. Only the back reclined; the seat did not move. Still, it was one of the most comfortable chairs of the time. The back and the seat were cushioned in leather, and it almost always had a matching footstool. The chair was quite roomy and served as a focal point in many rooms. Its utility, comfort, simplicity, and quality craftsmanship has made it a symbol of Stickley's work and the Arts and Crafts movement.

Other Fine Craftsmen

Although Stickley's designs helped define Craftsman furniture, other fine designers and craftsmen were also producing beautiful and useful works of art. Some, like architects Wright and the Greene brothers, designed custom furniture for each client and for a specific spot in a house. Wright's designs were less rustic and homey than Stickley's. He was concerned primarily with a piece's function and how the furniture defined the architectural space and unified the overall design. Wright writes of his designs: "They are all mere structural details in the completeness, heating apparatus, light fixtures, the very chairs, tables, [and] cabinets . . . are of the building itself . . . as the plaster on the walls or the tiles on the roof."[44]

Wright used furniture instead of walls as spatial dividers, which was a new design concept. Also, his designs often imitated the building's architectural features. In Robie House, a home Wright designed in 1908 for Chicago business executive Frederick Robie, Wright created a sofa with broad oak armrests that projected out like wings in the same way the house's roof projected over the building. Besides serving as a unifying design factor, the size and shape of the armrests eliminated the need for end tables.

Wright's furniture was strong, straight, and starkly geometrical. The Greene brothers' furniture had a softer appearance characterized by subtly rounded corners and edges. While Wright used machines to assist in the production of his designs, the Greenes' creations were entirely handcrafted. Each piece was made of the finest materials and was rich in small woodworking details. One detail that was common in their designs was the cloud lift, a rise in a horizontal line that is formed by two connecting arcs. The Greenes designed bold, large cloud lifts that altered the shape of the top of a chair, and they designed tiny cloud lifts that served as very subtle adornments.

The Greenes also used elements of structure as adornment. They left wood joinery exposed, turning *tenons* (projections on the edge of a piece of wood) and *mortises* (notches that tenons fit in) into design details. Sometimes, they added joinery for simple decoration even though it was not essential for structure. They often covered screws and nails with bits of decorative ebony.

What made all these small details important was how each one complemented the others. As Seattle furniture designer Darrell Peart remarks:

> While much of the magic of the Greene and Greene style lies in its details, those details, independent of each other, have little magic. Simply adding a spattering of great details to a piece does not by itself make

The furniture in Frank Lloyd Wright's winter home, Taliesin West in Arizona, demonstrates his love of function. The seats along the wall are built in to provide ample seating for guests without altering the balance of the room.

for a good design. They must be used judiciously, in context, and work with one another to create a unified vision. Charles Greene was a true master of this. It was his vision and artistic ability, for the most part, that brought together so many details to speak in a common language. The mature work of Greene and Greene always conveyed a strong, organic sense of unity.[45]

Making Furniture into an Art

Other Arts and Crafts furniture designers, like Charles Limbert (1854–1923), Charles Rohlfs (1853–1936), and the Roycrofters were not architects, but rather artists who created furniture. Rohlfs's designs were custom made, while Limbert and the Roycrofters designed furniture for production. Rohlfs was an actor before he started designing furniture as a hobby. Rohlfs's work was inspired by medieval designs. It was characterized by elaborate carving, which was more like the work produced by British Arts and Crafts-era designers than that of his American counterparts. In fact, in 1902 he designed a set of chairs for London's Buckingham Palace. Despite the more ornate character of his work, Rohlfs is considered part of the American Arts and Crafts movement because of his careful attention to detail, use of local materials, and the fine craftsmanship of his designs.

The work of Limbert and the Roycrofters was simpler and more like that of other American designers. Limbert started out as a salesman for a furniture manufacturing company in Grand Rapids, Michigan, before trying his hand at furniture design. His designs were constructed of large solid planks of wood without adornment other than decorative wood cutouts in the shape of squares, rectangles, and hearts. His work became so popular that in 1904, Limbert opened the Holland Dutch Arts and Crafts factory in Holland, Michigan. Here, he employed a number of craftspeople to build his furniture. In the arts and crafts tradition of utopian craft communities, Limbert provided his workers with houses and recreational facilities.

Members of the utopian Roycroft craftsman community were also well known for their extremely plain handcrafted oak and maple furniture. Elbert Hubbard, the founder of the community, developed a method of staining wood by soaking it in water containing rusty nails. This gave Roycroft furniture a rich, reddish luster. Roycroft furniture was further distinguished by the word Roycroft prominently inscribed in large Gothic letters across the back of many pieces, and/or a trademark R in a

Roycroft furniture, recognizable by its reddish color, is known for its hand-made quality.

ART NOUVEAU

Art nouveau literally means new art. The Art Nouveau movement was an art movement that arose from the Arts and Crafts movement. It aimed at modernizing design and was popular from 1890 to 1914. Some Arts and Crafts artists such as designer Louis Comfort Tiffany and architect Louis Sullivan were linked to both movements.

Like the Arts and Crafts movement, the Art Nouveau movement encompassed architecture, furniture, textiles, lighting, silverware, jewelry, paintings, and graphic arts. Followers of Art Nouveau believed that all art should be beautiful and spiritually uplifting. They also believed the function of an object should follow its form. Art Nouveau designs were characterized by long, graceful curvy lines. Tall curving tulips and lilies, women with long flowing hair, peacocks, willow leaves, intertwined ocean waves, and wispy clouds are commonly depicted in Art Nouveau designs. Art Nouveau designers embraced the use of machines in their work, and Art Nouveau was the first commercial art form used to improve the beauty of manufactured objects.

circle below a double barred cross. According to Dard Hunter (1883–1966), a Roycroft craftsman, [the furniture is] "the most beautiful because it is the simplest furniture, and is made by artists and not by mechanics and machines. It is solid and just what it appears to be—no shams, no veneer."[46]

Honest, simple, functional, finely crafted furniture that mirrored the clean lines of the house was a hallmark of the American Arts and Crafts movement. Warm wood that connected one room to the next, handcrafted tiles, and hearths added to the welcoming atmosphere. For the designers of the Arts and Crafts movement, designing a home was much like painting a picture. Their concern for beauty, harmony, and unity of design turned buildings into artistic masterpieces.

4

Decorative Arts

Many talented craftspeople were part of the Arts and Crafts movement. Finely crafted pottery, art glass, metal work, and textiles provided the finishing touches to Arts and Crafts homes.

Lighting up the Home

Light and its effect on indoor space were very important to Arts and Crafts-era designers. Architects like Frank Lloyd Wright and the Greene brothers considered custom lighting part of their home design. Wright used both outdoor and indoor light to create a feeling of warmth in his buildings. He considered glaring direct light too harsh; filtered light created the softer feeling he preferred. Wright wrote that he wanted light in his buildings to appear in the same way as "sunlight sifts through leaves in the trees."[47]

To soften the sunlight that streamed into a room, Wright designed light screens, windows, and skylights made of *art glass*. Art glass is a term that describes decorated glass that uses color, texture, and form for its appeal. Cut glass and stained glass are forms of art glass. To create art glass, craftspeople cut

A Greene-designed ceiling light uses slag glass to diffuse the light and is adorned with a bird for an element of nature.

glass into different shapes and then form the glass pieces into a design held together with metal strips. The glass with various textures changes the effect of light. For instance, bumpy textured colored glass produces a jewel-like glow when light passes through it.

Wright's light screens were constructed of colored, clear, or iridescent glass set in linear patterns. These patterns were often abstractions of natural elements like plants. One of Wright's most famous designs is a geometric prairie sumac plant; another is his geometric Tree of Life design. To provide design unity, Wright echoed the pattern on art glass lamp shades, back-lit ceiling panels, and chandeliers elsewhere in the room.

The Greene brothers also used art glass in their lighting. They were especially skilled at using light fixtures to create unity between the outside landscape and the interior of a house. For example, in their 1907 Blacker House in Pasadena,

California, they created art glass lanterns decorated with stained glass lilies just like the lilies in a pond outside the house. Light from the lanterns reflected off a ceiling adorned with a mural of the lily pond. When the light hit the gold leaf (gold that is beaten into thin sheets) in the mural, it created the illusion of shimmering ripples on the water. "The lamps are more important for the effects they produce than for their presence as separate objects,"[48] says Ellen Knell, the current owner of Blacker House.

Louis Comfort Tiffany Experiments with Glass

Artist Louis Comfort Tiffany (1848–1933) was also concerned with light. He created detailed stained glass windows, panels, and lampshades that have become symbols of the Arts and Crafts and the preceding Art Nouveau movement. The latter celebrated beauty in all forms and was characterized by the use of curving lines. Tiffany attended art school in New York and Paris. He worked in every artistic medium, but he is best known for his work in glass.

Tiffany began experimenting with glass in 1875. He conducted experiments in which he exposed molten glass to various chemicals in an effort to change the glass's color and texture. Over a period of twenty years, Tiffany developed four new types of glass characterized by vibrant colors and interesting textures. The most famous is *Favrile*, a word Tiffany coined based on an old English word that means handcrafted. Favrile is pearlescent glass with subtle streaks of different colors running through it, much like an opal gemstone. It was different from other colored glass of the time because the color was embedded in the glass rather than painted on the surface. Some of the colors in Favrile glass included gold, turquoise, red, and green.

Tiffany created elaborate vases, lamp shades, windows, and glass panels with Favrile glass. His stained glass windows and panels are regarded as masterpieces. One of his most famous pieces was a floor to ceiling panel of red, white, and blue stained glass surrounding an oval shield with eagles, which stood in the entrance hall of the White House for many years.

Tiffany's wisteria design stained-glass window for Laurelton Hall, his own home in Long Island, New York, is another stunning piece. Wisteria is a climbing vine with hanging clusters of lush blue-purple flowers. Tiffany designed the window to echo

Artist Louis Comfort Tiffany is best known for his works in stained glass. He created the wisteria stained-glass design (below) for his own home in New York.

the wisteria that draped the exterior walls of the house. The stained-glass wisteria is so detailed and the variation of color of each leaf and blossom so natural that it is hard to distinguish the glass flowers from the real ones.

Tiffany's stained-glass lampshades were also considered works of art. He and artists he supervised created more than three hundred different lampshade designs featuring floral, bird, insect, and geometric subjects. The shades topped sculptural bases, which often repeated the design theme. For example, as an article on the Metropolitan Museum of Art's website states: "A water lily lamp with its organic bronze support composed of lily pads, is crowned by a shade featuring pink opalescent stems that terminate in creamy water lily blossoms."[49]

Once a design was created, it was traced onto a pattern and used for hundreds of lamps. This made Tiffany's art affordable for people at every economic level. Even though the lamps were not custom made, the colors and textures of the glass in each lamp were slightly different, making each piece unique.

The Glittery Appeal of Hammered Copper

Another master craftsman named Dirk van Erp (1860–1933) was also making unique lamps that brought a soft glow to Arts and Crafts homes. Van Erp was a coppersmith who worked at a naval yard in San Francisco, California. There he gathered discarded shell casings from which he made candlesticks, vases, and lamps. His work became so popular that he opened his own shop in 1904 where he produced hammered copper lamps with translucent mica shades. Mica is a tawny colored mineral that can be formed into thin sheets. When it is struck by light, it has a glittery appearance.

Van Erp handcrafted every piece. To create his lamp bases, he heated flat sheets of copper, which he hammered until the metal *raised*, or formed, the walls for the lamp's base. He hand-rolled the raised copper into a conical shape and soldered it together.

Then, using a special hammer, he finished the piece, texturing and forming it into shapes that resembled milk cans, bean pots, bullets, and trumpets. Van Erp also hand-rolled copper to form the rim and cap of his lampshades, as well as the straps between the mica panels. When lit, van Erp's lamps produced a soft amber glow that complemented the fiery copper base.

Because they were made completely by hand, van Erp's creations were expensive. Yet, they were very popular. Their simplicity of design and fine handcraftsmanship made these lamps symbols of the Arts and Crafts movement. As art blogger Paula Scher writes: "Even today when somebody wants a handsome photograph of Arts and Crafts furniture, they'll put a van Erp lamp on the Mission table and plug it in."[50]

Yellin Creates Wrought Iron Masterpieces

Metal was also the medium of choice of another famous American artist, Samuel Yellin (1885–1940). Yellin was born in Poland, where he learned to work with iron. When he immigrated to Pennsylvania in 1906, he was already a highly skilled craftsman. Nevertheless, he studied metal work at the Philadelphia Museum School of Industrial Arts; within a year, he was teaching at the school, and a few years later he became an American citizen.

Before the Industrial Revolution, craftsmen used a hammer and an anvil to shape fiery hot iron into beautiful designs. Iron objects formed in this manner are known as wrought or hammered iron. Innovations brought about by the Industrial Revolution made it possible to shape and create designs in iron by heating the metal in patterned molds, a technique known as *cast iron*. Although many cast iron objects are beautiful, they lack the individuality, hand-hammered finish, and the fine details of wrought iron. Yellin was instrumental in reviving the older way of working with iron. In 1909, he opened Samuel Yellin Metalworkers in Philadelphia, where he and a staff of more than

Samuel Yellin hand-crafted beautiful and functional works of art, such as this detailed window grille, from wrought iron.

two hundred craftspeople created finely detailed hand-wrought iron gates, fireplace screens, window grates, and door knockers, pulls, and knobs, among other objects. Yellin was inspired by the old ironwork he had seen in Europe. He used the older designs as jumping off points from which he created new designs that reflected the time he lived in. Yellin advised other metal artists "[to avoid] a slavish imitation or repetition of old things, which were created in a different age, under entirely different circumstances."[51]

To create his wrought iron pieces, Yellin and his staff first made detailed drawings of their designs, which Yellin had to approve before work could begin. Although the drawings were excellent guides, the finished products rarely duplicated the initial designs. Working with metal inspired Yellin. As he details: "We made . . . many detailed drawings, but when I began to work them on the anvil, they shaped themselves quite differently from the way they appeared in the original sketches. The creative spirit . . . like a winged thing . . . must have freedom in which to sing and soar."[52]

The results were pieces created with simple but graceful details like intertwined leaves and branches, animal heads, birds in flight, and exquisite arched grille work. Yellin paid scrupulous attention to detail, whether he was forging a small door pull or a massive gate like the one he made for the Federal Reserve Bank of New York City, which required 200 tons of wrought iron. Although Yellin modestly referred to himself simply as a "metal worker," art historians consider him a genius. He set the standard in design and craftsmanship for metal artists of his time as well as for those who followed.

Art from the Earth

Other gifted craftspeople used clay to make simple, finely-crafted pottery. At a time when women did not typically own businesses or work as professional artists, a number of women were finding employment in the field of ceramics. One of the most successful was Maria Longworth Nichols Storer (1849–1932), who established, owned, and operated Rookwood Pottery in Cincinnati, Ohio. Storer was a member of one of the wealthiest families in Cincinnati and studied art and music as a child. As a young woman, she took up china painting (painting designs on white china), a popular hobby for wealthy women at that time. After seeing an exhibit of pottery at the 1876 Centennial Exhibition in Philadelphia, she began experimenting with designing and making pottery. She was especially interested in ceramic glazes. A glaze is a liquid that is applied to clay and then heated at high temperatures to form a hard surface. Glazes are composed of various compounds that impart color and texture to the surface of clay objects. Glazes can be clear, colored, glossy, or matte (dull). More than one glaze can be applied to a pot's surface.

Storer developed a number of glazes including high gloss deep yellow, orange and red glazes, a textured sea green matte

GEORGE OHR

George Ohr (1857–1918), also known as "The Mad Potter of Biloxi," and "the Picasso of Pottery," may be the most innovative potter of the Arts and Crafts era. Ohr made handmade pottery from bright red, local clay in astonishingly bright color combinations and odd abstract shapes that had never been seen before. As author Bruce Watkins writes in *Smithsonian* magazine:

> Just as Cézanne was breaking up the plane of the painter's canvas, Ohr was shattering the conventions of ceramic. He made pitchers whose open tops resembled yawning mouths. He threw slim, multi-tiered vases with serpentine handles. He lovingly shaped bowls into symmetrical forms, then crumpled them as if to thumb his nose at the art world. He fired his works into kaleidoscopic colors.

Ohr did not achieve great success during his life, but he insisted his work would be celebrated in the future. He was right. His work is exhibited at the Smithsonian Institution, New York's Metropolitan Museum of Art, and the Ohr-O'Keefe Museum in Biloxi, Mississippi—the United States' first museum dedicated to a single potter.

Bruce Watkins. "The Mad Potter of Biloxi." *Smithsonian*, February 2004. www.smithsonianmag.com/arts -culture/biloxi.html.

glaze, a velvety pale blue matte glaze, and a brown glaze flecked with bits of gold. She also did extensive work with under and overglazes. An underglaze is applied to a piece before other glazes. It is used to create designs and patterns that show through the overglaze, the glaze that covers the design. Storer's interest in underglazes was so strong that she had a special kiln built just for her experiments with underglazes. From this, Rookwood Pottery was born.

Rookwood Pottery employed potters who threw, or shaped, the pottery, and fired the pottery and ceramic designers who designed and decorated the pots, each of which varied in shape, color, and decoration. Rookwood Pottery was known for its fine quality vases, bowls, and other ceramic objects. Staying true to the principles of the Arts and Crafts movement, Storer used only local clay. She also insisted on high quality standards. As a result, Rookwood designs won more than one hundred international awards and made Storer one of the most celebrated female artists of the time.

Women Work with Clay

Women artists were also instrumental in the pottery produced by the Pewabic Pottery company and the Newcomb Pottery studio. The artist Mary Chase Perry Stratton (1867–1961) founded Pewabic Pottery in 1903 in Detroit, Michigan. Stratton grew up on the Upper Peninsula of Michigan. One of Mary's childhood pastimes was forming little figures with the copper-colored clay that is found there. As she explains:

> I suppose the beginning of my idea [of becoming a ceramic artist and starting Pewabic Pottery] . . . dates back to the time when as a little girl, near Lake Superior, I found clay which could be used for modeling and entertained myself by fashioning figures and designs, which were later fired in a brick yard, much to my delight. I loved working with clay. . . . Ever since, I have been trying to develop the resources of America by using the clays found in our soil.[53]

Like Storer, Stratton was interested in ceramic glazes. Her next door neighbor, Horace James Caulkins, happened to be a dentist who had a kiln that he used to make false teeth. He

The iridescent, rainbow-like, glaze on this vase is the signature look of Pewabic Pottery, founded by Mary Chase Perry Stratton in 1903.

allowed Stratton to use the kiln to experiment with glazes. She worked tirelessly mixing chemicals in hopes of developing an iridescent glaze. When her experiments failed to produce the effect she wanted, she had Caulkins build a kiln that produced extremely high heat, hoping it would yield better results, which it did. Eventually the two became partners in the Pewabic Pottery company. Pewabic means copper-colored in the Chippewa language. The copper-colored clay came from an area that was home to Chippewa Indians.

Stratton was both an artist and a chemist. She carefully painted designs on her work, and she mixed all the glazes herself, keeping records of her recipes in a notebook. She developed

ART THERAPY

Followers of the Arts and Crafts movement believed that art could change society in positive ways. In 1905, Dr. Herbert Hall established a pottery workshop in Marblehead, Massachusetts, as a way to provide therapy for female patients with nervous disorders at a nearby mental hospital. He hired Alfred Baggs, a ceramic artist, to run the workshop. However, the work was too difficult for the patients. In 1915, Baggs bought the pottery workshop, which was known as Marblehead Pottery, and hired six professional ceramic artists to work with him including Sarah Tutt, who was the principal designer.

Marblehead pottery reflected the seaside location of Marblehead. All the pots were handmade and beautifully crafted. They were simply shaped and softly colored in shades of matte blue, green, sandy yellow, and gray, much like the colors of the surrounding landscape. Marine decorations including fish, sailboats, seahorses, sea birds, and seaweed were common motifs.

The company remained in business until 1936. Marblehead pottery is highly prized today by collectors of Arts and Crafts-era ceramics.

a number of glazes. The most famous is an iridescent glaze that glittered with multiple colors, producing a rainbow-like effect. The glaze became the trademark of Pewabic Pottery.

The company produced lamps, vases, bowls, and architectural tiles. Pewabic ceramic tiles and decorative objects are still found in buildings throughout Michigan, as well as in the Basilica of the National Shrine of the Immaculate Conception in Washington, D.C. There, Stratton designed a tall archway

Newcomb Pottery trained women in the art of ceramic design. All pots were handmade and reflected the local environment.

outlined in iridescent tiles. Pewabic pottery is also on exhibit in the Louvre Museum in Paris and the Detroit Institute of Arts.

Women were also instrumental in the work produced by Newcomb Pottery, which was founded in 1895 as a women's college in association with Tulane University in New Orleans. Under the direction of artist Ellsworth Woodward (1861–1939) and designer Mary Given Sheerer (1865–1954), women were trained in ceramic design and decoration with the goal of providing a skill that would allow them to support themselves. As part of their training, the students worked at the company along with male potters who threw and fired the pots. Graduates could continue to work at Newcomb Pottery as independent ceramicists. Over the years, a total of about ninety graduates stayed on. Many became well-known designers, including Sadie Irvine, Sarah Henderson, Henrietta Bailey, and Harriet Joor.

Following Arts and Crafts ideals, Newcomb pots reflected the local landscape and environment. The clay was gathered locally, and the designs on the pieces were inspired by local plant life such as magnolia blossoms, pine cones, cotton bolls, and moss-draped cypress trees. The pottery was best known for its soft blue and green colors. Often the color was applied as an underglaze, which was then topped by a clear matte overglaze. All Newcomb pots were handmade, and no two were identical. Each designer signed her work with a private design or monogram.

Grueby's Shades of Green

Many of the pots created by American ceramicists could not have had a dull or matte glaze if not for William H. Grueby (1867–1925), a potter and the founder of the Grueby Faience Company. Grueby began working in an art tile company in Boston when he was only thirteen years old. He worked there for ten years, during which time he was encouraged to experiment with glazes. In 1894, he opened his own ceramics company, Grueby Faience, while continuing his experiments. Grueby's goal was to develop an opaque matte glaze that could be applied to clay in the same manner as a glossy glaze. Until then, the only way to achieve the matte effect was to sandblast the glossy pottery or treat it with acid.

By 1897, Grueby was exhibiting vases, lamp bases, art tiles, and decorative ceramic pots with an opaque matte glaze in varying shades of green. He called the glaze *faience*. As writer and art pottery collector, Steve Fales details:

Opaque, often thick and typically of low luster, Grueby "green" ranged from a dark, rich, and relatively even finish to all manner of highly complex curdled, crackled, veined speckled, and even crystalline effects. A single superior example, studied close-up, might carry virtually every shade of the color, from black/green spots and flecks to a soft yellow where the glaze eased away from high points to reveal the underlying clay.[54]

Working with designer George Prentiss Kendrick (1850–1919), who decorated Grueby's pots with simple floral designs, Grueby created ceramic pieces that exemplified the Arts and Crafts movement in their simplicity, plain shapes, subdued glaze, muted color, high quality, and handcraftsmanship. Grueby also created art tiles for Gustav Stickley, who used the tiles on his tabletops. Indeed, Stickley and Grueby often exhibited their work together at joint exhibitions and trade fairs. Grueby eventually employed many craftspeople. Although the company often used the same design on multiple pieces, each piece was thrown by hand. The work was so popular that more than one hundred ceramic companies imitated Grueby's faience glaze and simple style.

Textiles Provide a Finishing Touch

Original designs were also the hallmark of textiles, which, in the form of table linens, curtains, wall hangings, bedspreads, and pillows, provided the finishing touch to Arts and Crafts décor. Stickley was also instrumental in promoting and defining textiles that appropriately complemented Craftsman style homes and furniture. He popularized the use of rustic, natural colored cloth such as canvas, burlap, and linen. As he explains: "What we needed were fabrics that possessed sturdiness and durability; that were made of materials that possess a certain rugged and straightforward character of fiber, weave and texture—such a

The rise of the Arts and Crafts movement in the United States was accompanied by an appreciation for traditional Native American handcrafts. Hand-woven Navajo blankets were especially prized. The Navajo people had been raising sheep, harvesting the animal's wool, and weaving the wool into beautiful blankets for centuries.

Traditionally, Navajo men built the looms, and women wove blankets with bold geometric designs that symbolized the natural world. The designs were based on the Navajo principles of balance, harmony, beauty, and goodness.

Navajo weavings appealed to followers of the Arts and Crafts movement for many reasons. First, they were useful, handcrafted objects. Second, in the spirit of the Arts and Crafts movement, Navajo weavers integrated art and labor into their daily life. Finally, the bold geometric designs harmonized well with the simple furniture and handmade decorative items of the era. The blankets were used as rugs, wall hangings, and bed covers in Arts and Crafts-era homes and are valued at thousands of dollars today.

character as would bring them into the same class as the sturdy oak and wrought iron and copper of the other furnishings."[55]

The cloth was decorated with simple designs, which were applied either in the form of embroidery or *appliqué*, a process in which a design is cut out of fabric and then sewn onto a base material. Floral decorations featuring local plants like roses, gingko plants, pine cones, magnolias, and grapes were most popular. They helped bring the outdoors inside and integrate

This linen table runner is an example of the kinds of textiles that complement the Arts and Crafts décor.

the home with its environment. Often the same motif would be used throughout the home, creating design unity. It might also appear in art tiles, rugs, wall stencils, stained glass lampshades, and ceramic pieces.

In addition to producing textiles, Stickley used his publication *The Craftsman* to promote embroidery and hand appliqué work as hobbies. Many Arts and Crafts-era homes featured table linens and pillow covers lovingly embroidered by family members. The Roycrofters and students at Newcomb College also produced hand-embroidered textiles.

There is no doubt that the Arts and Crafts movement inspired many talented artists to create simple, useful, and finely-crafted decorative objects that added beauty and warmth to Arts and Crafts homes. The innovations and vision of people like Grueby, Stratton, Tiffany, and Yellin gave decorative objects associated with the Arts and Crafts movement long lasting reputations for beauty and value.

The Arts and Crafts Revival

The popularity of the Arts and Crafts movement declined at the start of World War I (1914–1918). After the war, growing interest in the new modernist art movement lessened public enthusiasm for fine craftsmanship. Modernists embraced all of the changes brought about by industrialism. They celebrated machine made, mass-produced objects as a form of art and rejected traditional handcrafted items.

Although interest in the Arts and Crafts movement did not entirely disappear, it was reduced even further by the tough economic times of the Great Depression in the 1930s. Many Arts and Crafts designers closed their shops, and some, like Gustav Stickley, were forced to declare bankruptcy.

"Ideas Come Full Circle"

World War II preoccupied American minds for most of the 1940s. After the war, industrial production increased significantly, and with it, the popularity of the modernist art movement. Arts and Crafts-era homes and décor were considered old-fashioned and of little value. Before his death in 1915, Elbert Hubbard had predicted that interest in the Arts and

Crafts movement would die out and then reemerge in the future: "Ideas come full circle. And then they come again," he opined. "And this death and resurrection goes on forever."[56]

Hubbard's prediction was correct. Although it seemed as if the Arts and Crafts movement were dead, a 1972 Princeton University exhibit titled "American Arts and Crafts: 1876–1916" generated renewed interest in the movement. Other exhibits followed, restoring respect for Arts and Crafts-era artwork. The technological revolution of the 1980s and 1990s also affected the Arts and Crafts revival. Like the Industrial Revolution, the technological revolution changed the way people lived and worked. Reaction to the way technology was replacing the work of humans led to renewed interest in Arts and Crafts ideals. As Kitty Turgeon, an artist who has spearheaded the Arts and Crafts revival details: "The cycle that gave birth to Arts and Crafts is being repeated. Arts and Crafts was a reaction to the machine. Today it's the computer. It's the same thing."[57]

In the St. Petersburg, Florida, area the Arts and Crafts style has remained popular over the years. Even the local Walmart building incorporates references to the Arts and Crafts bungalow style.

Today Arts and Crafts-era homes, furniture, and decorative objects are in great demand, and many modern architects and designers have embraced the principles of the Arts and Crafts movement. Some are restoring old objects and homes; others are creating reproductions of Arts and Crafts-era designs, while others are creating innovative contemporary pieces based on Arts and Crafts principles.

The Best of Both Worlds

The Arts and Crafts revival has inspired many homeowners to restore Arts and Crafts-era homes. This can be a daunting task. After World War II (1941–1945), many owners of Arts and Crafts-era homes renovated buildings based on design trends that conflicted with Arts and Crafts ideals. It was common to tear out built-in furniture, build walls over fireplaces, paint or paper over interior wood and art tile, hide wood ceiling beams under dropped ceilings, cover exterior woodwork with aluminum siding or stucco, cover wood floors with linoleum, close off sleeping porches, remove art glass fixtures and windows, replace wood window frames with aluminum, and build on rooms that were out of character with the rest of the building. In addition, Arts and Crafts-era furniture, art tiles, and handcrafted decorative items were discarded and replaced with machine-made goods. At the same time, movement of Americans from the cities to the suburbs left neglected Arts and Crafts homes in deteriorating urban neighborhoods. Many Arts and Crafts homes were divided up and turned into boarding houses and small apartment buildings. Others were abandoned.

The Arts and Crafts revival brought about renewed interest in these homes. In the course of renovating the buildings, many new owners make every effort to maintain the home's original character. This often involves restoring the original features whenever possible. If this is impossible, new designs are based on Arts and Crafts principles. Chris Wilson, the owner of a 1909 Portland, Oregon bungalow, writes:

EXPLORING OAK PARK, ILLINOIS

Oak Park, Illinois, is the home of more than two dozen buildings designed by Frank Lloyd Wright. Wright lived in Oak Park, which is located west of Chicago, from 1889 to 1909. It was here that he developed Prairie Style architecture.

Wright's home in Oak Park still stands. He designed both the home and the work studio inside it. About eighty thousand people visit there each year. Guides lead visitors on tours through the house, which is decorated with furniture also designed by Wright. The guides point out interesting features, such as the way Wright manipulated space. For instance, his studio appears much larger than it actually is because of a small passageway that opens up inside the room and creates the illusion of size. In the playroom, Wright cut a hole in a wall and placed a piano in the hole. All that can be seen of the piano is the keys. The body of the piano hangs over a stairwell, filling up a space that would otherwise be wasted.

Touring the town itself is also interesting. In addition to the buildings designed by Wright, his designs are incorporated in area mailboxes, windows, doors, and street lamps.

I restored what woodwork I could and matched its simplicity where I had to add it . . . . Starting on the exterior, I removed the imitation brick siding (1958), then primed and painted the clapboards underneath in a schoolhouse green, which was evident behind a cornerboard . . . . I replaced the front steps, stripped the front and back doors, and added appropriately modest period hardware where it was missing . . . . Fortunately, the chandeliers in the parlor and dining room were still there and just needed a thorough cleaning. In the kitchen, I took up the vinyl floor and just waxed the wood underneath.[58]

Other owners make changes to the buildings to better suit modern lifestyles. Making sure these changes harmonize with the original design helps maintain the home's charm. As Michigan architect Michael Klement says: "There's no reason why a renovation can't solve . . . space-planning problems. Using period-style details doesn't preclude a contemporary use of the space."[59]

Early-twentieth-century kitchens were much smaller than modern kitchens and lacked modern appliances. "We don't use kitchens today the way we did in 1915," writes author Patricia

The living room of a 1913 Arts and Crafts home in Detroit, Michigan, had fallen into disrepair until new homeowners did a full restoration in the 2000s.

Poore. "Rather than a service room, the kitchen has become a public center of the house, outfitted more like a living and dining room. In renovations, the original kitchen is often made larger and is opened up to the rest of the house."[60]

Changes by former owners often made matters worse. In Mary Kennedy's 1913 Seattle bungalow, a previous owner had partitioned off part of the kitchen to build a bathroom, significantly reducing the size of the already small kitchen. "The kitchen was almost too horrible to describe," she says. "We could basically fit one person in there to cook, and in order to open the spice drawer, you had to first open the door to the stove!"[61] Working with a designer who specializes in updating homes while maintaining the original style and craftsmanship, Kennedy enlarged the kitchen and added modern appliances. The addition of a built-in breakfast nook, countertops made of natural materials, a rustic farmhouse sink, and vintage light fixtures provided design unity and preserved the room's Arts and Crafts character.

Preserving Historic Neighborhoods

Many beautifully restored Arts and Crafts homes are clustered together in historic neighborhoods throughout the country. Some of these neighborhoods have been identified as historic or landmark districts by the local, state, and/or federal government. Some are listed in the National Register of Historic Places. Placement on the National Register of Historic Places is an honorary designation given to neighborhoods whose historical, cultural, and architectural significance are part of the nation's cultural heritage. Buildings in a historic district are recognized for their architectural and landscape design, attention to detail, and fine craftsmanship. The designation acknowledges the need to preserve the historic qualities of the area. It discourages residents from destroying, neglecting, or altering the character of the buildings.

Patrons wait for a trolley during the 2012 BungalowFest, an annual tour of historic homes, many of which are Arts and Crafts style, in St. Petersburg, Florida.

One memorable historic district is Bungalow Heaven in Pasadena, California. It is comprised of more than one thousand carefully preserved Craftsman-style bungalows built between 1905 and 1925. With its peaceful streets and beautifully restored homes, the neighborhood seems to be part of a calmer, gentler time. "You will find tree-canopied streets, quiet sidewalks, well-kept houses, a quiet, homey community where neighbors stand on front lawns to talk to each other," states an article in a Japanese magazine. "There is a sense of warmth and peacefulness on these streets, a feeling of community."[62]

Bungalow Heaven is such an attractive community that the neighborhood was designated one of the ten great places in the United States by the American Planning Association, an organization involved in community development. In an effort to share the neighborhood's artistic and cultural history, the residents of Bungalow Heaven sponsor a neighborhood walking tour once a year. Some residents dress in period clothes and allow visitors to tour their homes, which are decorated with restored Arts and Crafts-era furniture and decorative objects, as well as finely crafted modern objects that blend well with the homes. Tourists come from all over the world to attend the event.

Other historic districts featuring lovingly preserved Arts and Crafts-era homes can be found in Newport News, Virginia; St. Paul, Minnesota; Palo Alto and Berkeley, California; Portland, Oregon; Indianapolis, Indiana; Tampa and St. Petersburg, Florida; Oak Park, Illinois; and Dallas and Fort Worth, Texas, among others.

Modern Interpretations

In addition to restoring Arts and Crafts-era homes, some contemporary architects specialize in designing new homes based on Arts and Crafts principles. These homes are constructed of natural local materials, have open floor plans, lots of natural light, feature fine craftsmanship and simple designs, offer ample outdoor living space, and harmonize with the local landscape. Architect Matthew Bialecki describes the Arts and Crafts-inspired homes he designs: "Plans are open, materials are raw stone or wood, rooms open to the landscape with large glass walls, and handcrafted details abound uniting the spaces in a common vocabulary."[63]

In keeping with the Arts and Crafts philosophy of appreciation for nature and the environment, many contemporary Arts and Crafts homes incorporate sustainable or green building concepts into their design. According to the U.S. Green Building Council, the goal of green building design is: "to significantly reduce or eliminate the negative impact of buildings on the environment and on the building occupants. Green building design and construction practices address: sustainable site planning, safeguarding water and water efficiency, energy efficiency, conservation of materials and resources, and indoor environmental quality."[64] Many of these homes are LEED (Leadership in Energy and Environmental Design) certified. LEED certification indicates that a building meets green building design standards.

With these concepts and the principles of the Arts and Crafts movement in mind, a contemporary green home inspired by the Arts and Crafts movement is usually sited to best control the effects of heat, wind, and cold on the home. For instance, buildings that face south and southwest garner the most passive solar energy, which helps warm the home, thereby conserving energy. Double-paned windows and extra insulation also help keep the building's temperature comfortable. In addition, the building is likely to have solar panels with photovoltaic cells to generate electricity and heat water. Energy star appliances, the designation given to energy saving appliances, also save energy.

Native landscaping, too, is common. It not only harmonizes with the environment, it tolerates local weather conditions and requires less maintenance and watering. Low-flow faucets and shower heads, low-flush toilets, and appliances designed to use less water also conserve water. According to an article on EcoFriend, a website dedicated to promoting green living, "Buildings account for 12 percent of total water consumption in the United States. By using low flow faucets and water heads, water sense or energy star clothes washers and dish washers, dual flush or low flow toilets and drought resistant and native landscaping . . . in your Craftsman style homes, you will be able to save a good amount of water."[65]

The materials used in the home are also chosen with the environment in mind. Wood is an important part of Arts and Crafts homes. Arts and Crafts-style green homes use sustainable wood harvested from forests that are carefully managed to prevent damage to eco-systems. Recycled wood that has been reclaimed from old buildings or furniture is also used frequently. Other recycled building materials are also popular. Low or no-VOC (volatile organic compounds) paint is also preferred. Paint contains as many as one thousand chemicals, many of which are harmful. VOCs cause indoor air pollution and have been linked to cancer. Low or no-VOC paint contains fewer or no volatile organic compounds, which makes them healthier and better for the environment.

Author Regina Cole describes a LEED certified Arts and Crafts-style home in Maryland:

> The house, which has bungalow-era and Prairie-style details, was designed by noted bungalow revivalist Christian Gladu of Bend, Oregon . . . . From the insulated foundation to the rooftop solar panels, the . . . [house] embodies modern energy efficiency. Although LEED certification dates only to 2008, the philosophy is familiar to students of the Arts and Crafts movement and its revival. In the 'Incredibly Green Home,' the idea resulted in the use of mold-resistant drywall, cabinets constructed from American cherry certified [sustainable wood] by the Forest Stewardship Council,

A neo–Arts-and-Crafts–style home built in 2007 is based on the old-fashioned principles of the movement but updated with twenty-first century efficiencies.

materials with sources close to home, glass re-used from old windows, low-VOC paint, and recycled-fiber carpeting.[66]

Valuable Objects

The Arts and Crafts revival has also renewed interest in hand-crafted objects made during the era of the Arts and Crafts movement. Some individuals are fortunate enough to find Arts and Crafts-era pottery, tiles, lamps, stained glass, tapestries, or furniture at garage sales or stored away in attics. As interest in Arts and Crafts-era objects has increased, so has their value and people's desire to acquire them. Many pieces are displayed in museums, and many private individuals have become collectors. Celebrities like Brad Pitt, Barbra Streisand, Steven Spielberg, and Bruce Willis are among the most well-known Arts and Crafts collectors. In fact, in the 1980s, Streisand paid $363,000 for a Stickley sideboard, a type of cupboard used for storing dishes. She also paid $45,000 for a Tiffany lamp. As Streisand details: "I love when something stands the test of time, when it is so beautifully made you just have to stare at it. I remember thinking, 'How could I ever have spent $45,000 for a Tiffany lamp?' But you look at it, and that just cannot be duplicated today. God is in the details, to me."[67]

Other collectors have paid even more for original Tiffany lamps, which can fetch more than 1 million dollars. According to Tiffany expert Alistair Duncan: "The market for Tiffany lamps is very bright, even luminescent. It's a very strong market, which has suddenly turned up another notch. In fact, it has never been stronger."[68] Indeed, since a Japanese collector opened a private Tiffany Museum in 1994 and bought hundreds of the best examples of Tiffany's art, the demand far exceeds the supply.

Grueby and Rookwood pottery, too, are in great demand, selling for as much as $20,000 per pot. Van Erp lamps have fetched as much as $180,000. But art lovers do not have to be

EPHRAIM FAIENCE POTTERY

Wisconsin potter Kevin Hicks is the founder of Ephraim Faience Pottery, a modern pottery studio inspired by the Arts and Crafts movement. Ephraim Faience pottery is highly sought after. An article by Brian D. Coleman on the Arts and Crafts Homes and the Revival *magazine website describes the company:*

Kevin Hicks . . . opened his own pottery and embraced the philosophy of the Arts and Crafts movement with its emphasis on hand craftsmanship, individual creativity, and artistic expression. Influenced by early 20th–century potteries such as Grueby and Rookwood, Kevin and his partners nonetheless developed a style of their own, one strongly rooted in nature. Early on, gingko leaves and cattails, dragonflies and koi, bullfrogs and storks adorned pots and vases rendered in colors that reflect the seasons and the outdoors: maple-'Leaf Green,' quiet brown and gray 'Prairie Grass,' and 'Indigo' the deep color of the sky an hour after sunset.

Now Ephraim Faience Pottery has a staff of eleven that includes potters and sculptors, glazers and designers. . . . The pottery uses earthenware and stoneware clays from local Midwestern sources to make everything from cabinet vases and candlesticks to lanterns and umbrella stands. In true Arts and Crafts spirit, everything is made by hand.

Brian D. Coleman. "Ephraim Faience in the Studio." *Arts and Crafts Homes and the Revival*, February 16, 2012. http://artsandcraftshomes.com/ephraim-faience-in-the-studio.

rich to access beautiful Arts and Crafts-era objects. Pieces are displayed in museums throughout the United States, including New York's Metropolitan Museum of Art; the Los Angeles County Museum of Art; the Stickley Museum in Fayetteville,

A variety of original Tiffany lamps are on display at the Charles H. Morse Museum in Winter Park, Florida.

New York; the Dallas Museum of Art; and Winter Park, Florida's Morse Museum.

Modern Craftspeople

The Arts and Crafts revival has not only stimulated an interest in homes and decorative objects from the Arts and Crafts era, it has led to a newfound respect for handcrafted objects made by contemporary artists. Some are reproductions of older objects, while others are more innovative. Each is lovingly crafted by artists inspired by the Arts and Crafts movement.

Furniture designer Darrell Peart (b. 1950) of Seattle, Washington, is one of these contemporary craftsmen. Peart, considered one of the top furniture designers in the United States, is inspired by Charles and Henry Greene. He has designed and built more than one hundred pieces inspired by the Greene brothers. He has also written a workshop guidebook to creating Greene and Greene style furniture, and he gives woodworking classes.

Although Peart's work includes re-creations of Greene and Greene pieces, most of his designs are original. He uses elements of Greene and Greene design in his work and then innovates. Like the Greene brothers, his work is rich in small woodworking details. For instance, he often leaves wood joinery exposed, tops screws or nails with bits of ebony, uses cloud lifts in his designs, and highlights the wood's natural grain as part of the design. Yet, his work is still unique. An example is his Yuki No Hana (snow flower) table. The table's finely crafted mahogany legs and base form a complex six-sided snowflake pattern, which is visible through the *fused glass* table top that looks much like a crackled sheet of ice. Fused glass is a type of art glass in which two or more pieces of glass are heated at high temperature until they fuse together into a single piece. It has a bubbly, crackled appearance.

Peart does almost all the woodworking for his furniture himself. His favorite part of the process is designing the pieces. In an article in *Arts and Crafts Homes and the Revival* magazine, writer Mary Ellen Polson reports that Peart sees each piece of wood as a unique living part of nature and lets the wood's individual character guide his design. "These are not questions for intellect," he says. "We must call on our emotional nature for the answer—we must close our eyes and let our imagination and intuition play out the scenario."[69]

Other artists are inspired by the work of Ernest Batchelder. Arts and Crafts revival tile makers are creating modern reproductions of Batchelder's tiles and original tiles inspired by Batchelder's glazes and subject matter. Cha-Rie Tang, a Pasadena designer, uses molds from original Batchelder tiles to create contemporary reproductions of Batchelder's work. The tiles look much like the originals, but modern firing and glazing techniques make them more durable. As Tang explains:

> Years ago a friend found that his garden wall was made from Batchelder tiles. He was kind enough to allow me to make molds of his tiles. Since then I have been collecting Batchelder impressions

RENEGADE CRAFT FAIR

The Renegade Craft Fair (RCF) is a large craft fair that features the work of hundreds of promising craftspeople. As an article on the Renegade Craft Fair's website explains:

The inspiration for the Fair came about when the RCF founders wanted to take their hobbies to the next level and start participating in art and crafts shows. After looking into joining several events, it quickly became apparent that no event existed specifically to represent the emergent DIY [do-it-yourself] community of craftspeople and independent makers. These shows were much more geared towards 'fine art and craft,' and seemed to be seeking established artists rather than emerging young talent. RCF organizers imagined an alternative audience and different community of artisans for their events, which would feature more moderately priced goods of all kinds and cater towards a younger demographic interested in more contemporary designs. So, in 2003, the first Renegade Craft Fair was held in Chicago's Wicker Park featuring 75 vendors. With each year vendor and attendee interest grew and grew, new cities were added. . . . Today, RCF is widely regarded as a marquee event for the discovery of new talent.

"About." Renegade Craft Fair. www.renegadecraft.com/about.

and casting second-generation Batchelder tiles. Dr. Robert Winter, the author of *Batchelder Tilemaker*, gave me access to his whole collection in the Ernest Batchelder bungalow in Pasadena. He introduced me to the heirs of Ernest Batchelder, and I received their blessings to do these second generation tiles to keep the tradition alive.[70]

Other artists, like Robert Trout of New York, specialize in metal work. Trout makes hand-hammered copper art tiles, lamps, chandeliers, vases, picture frames, plates, and candlesticks. He is one of a group of talented craftspeople who have been designated a Roycroft Renaissance Master Artisan by the Roycrofters at Large Association. The association, formed in 1976, is a non-profit organization that works to keep the ideals of Elbert Hubbard and the Roycrofters alive. Roycroft Renaissance Artisans are carefully selected by the association based on skill and dedication to handcraftsmanship and include artists who work in wood, metal, glass, paper, and leather. As Trout details:

> One of the many famous Elbert Hubbard epigrams was 'head, heart, hands', signifying the Roycrofter's

A patron at the 2010 Arts and Crafts Festival in Syracuse, New York, admires handmade pottery on display.

emphasis on craftsmanship, design, and artistry in whatever was produced. As a Roycroft Renaissance Master Artisan in Metal, I seek to promote, preserve, and perpetuate the philosophy and skills exemplified in the Arts and Crafts movement through my own work.[71]

Thousands of talented craftspeople are producing beautiful handcrafted objects all over the world. Their work can be seen in craft fairs, art galleries, specialty shops, and design shows. Whether or not their designs reflect those produced by earlier artists like Stickley, Louis Comfort Tiffany, Samuel Yellin, Frank Lloyd Wright, or Batchelder, their dedication to fine craftsmanship has helped propel the Arts and Crafts movement into the twenty-first century.

Notes

Introduction: Beauty and Simplicity

1. Quoted in Elizabeth Cumming and Wendy Kaplan. *The Arts and Crafts Movement*. London: Thames and Hudson, 1991, p. 22.
2. Quoted in "William Morris Quotes." Brainy Quote. www.brainyquote .com/quotes/authors/w/william _morris.html.
3. Quoted in "Arts and Crafts Movement." Design Museum. http:// designmuseum.org/design/art-and -craft-movement.
4. Quoted in "William Morris Quotes." Brainy Quote.
5. Quoted in Pamela Todd. *Arts and Crafts Companion*. Bath, Great Britain: Palazzo Editions, 2004, p. 117.
6. Ken Lonsinger. "House Styles." Craftsman Perspective. www.craftsmanper spective.com/architecture/styles.html.
7. "The Arts and Crafts Movement." Colorado Arts and Crafts Society. www.coloarts-crafts.org/artsand craftshistory.htm.

Chapter 1: Social Reform Through Art

8. Quoted in Bruce Smith and Yoshiko Yamamoto. *The Beautiful Necessity*.

Layton, UT: Gibbs Smith, 1996, p. 23.
9. Quoted in Cumming and Kaplan. *The Arts and Crafts Movement*, p. 15.
10. Quoted in Wendy Kaplan. *The Arts and Crafts Movement in Europe and America*. New York: Thames and Hudson and Los Angeles: Los Angeles County Museum of Art, 2004, p. 27.
11. Ann Allen. "Red House." William Morris and Red House, 2003. www .morrisandredhouse.net/house.htm.
12. Quoted in Ann Allen. "The Garden of Red House." William Morris and Red House, 2003. www.morrisand redhouse.net/garden.htm.
13. Quoted in Cumming and Kaplan. *The Arts and Crafts Movement*, p.16.
14. Quoted in Charlotte Gere. "Morris and Company, 1861–1939." The Victorian Web. www.victorianweb .org/authors/morris/morisco.html.
15. Kaplan. *The Arts and Crafts Movement in Europe and America*, p. 34.
16. John Dando Sedding. *Art and Handicraft*. London: Paul, Trench, and Trubner, 1893, p. 56.
17. Quoted in Bruce Smith and Yoshiko Yamamoto. *The Beautiful Necessity*, p. 110.

18. Quoted in Raymond McInnis. *A History of the Amateur Woodworking Movement: A Decade-by-Decade Narrative of Amateur Woodworking in America from 1900 to 2000.* WoodworkingHistory.com. www.woodworkinghistory.com/chapter_2-2_magazines_manuals.htm.

19. Quoted in Todd. *Arts and Crafts Companion*, p. 22.

Chapter 2: "Buildings, Too, Are Children of the Earth"

20. Quoted in "Why Is Frank Lloyd Wright Important?" Frank Lloyd Wright All-Wright Site. www.fs-architects.com/pages/links/links.html.

21. Charles Keeler. *The Simple Home.* P. Elder, 1904.

22. Quoted in "Frank Lloyd Wright Quotations." Frank Lloyd Wright All-Wright Site. www.fs-architects.com/pages/links/links.html.

23. Quoted in Todd. *Arts and Crafts Companion*, p. 119.

24. "What Is Fallingwater?" Fallingwater. www.fallingwater.org/37/what-is-fallingwater.

25. Cumming and Wendy Kaplan. *The Arts and Crafts Movement*, p. 135.

26. James C. Massey and Shirley Maxwell. "A Craftsman Neighborhood in Portland, Oregon." *Old-House Journal*, August/September 2012. www.oldhouseonline.com/a-craftsman-neighborhood-in-portland-oregon.

27. Quoted in Lonsinger. "House Styles."

28. Quoted in "Architects Past and Present: Gustav Stickley." Aaroe Architectural, 2012. www.aaroearchitectural.com/architects-historic/95.

29. J.M. Edgar. "Arts and Crafts Styles: Craftsman, Prairie and Four-Square Architecture." Star Craft Custom Builders. http://starcraftcustombuilders.com/Architectural.Styles.ArtsAndCrafts.htm.

30. Quoted in "Greene and Greene Homes." The Arts and Crafts Society. www.arts-crafts.com/archive/acarchs/greene-greene-1.shtml.

31. Quoted in "Greene and Greene Homes."

32. Todd. *Arts and Crafts Companion*, p. 117.

33. Irving Gill. "The Home of the Future: The Architecture of the West: Small Homes for a Great Country." *The Craftsman*, May 1916, p. 143.

Chapter 3: Home, Hearth, and Family

34. Keeler. "The Simple Home."

35. Quoted in Smith and Yamamoto. *The Beautiful Necessity*, p. 100.

36. "A Family Fireplace." *The Craftsman*, June 1903, p. 201.

37. Jane Powell. "Heart of the Matter: A Look at the Wide Array of Arts and Crafts-Era Fireplaces." *Old House Journal*, March 2012, p. 22.

38. Quoted in "Four Definitions of His Life." Tile Nut. www.tilenut.com/Batchelder/Batchsynopsis.html.

39. Quoted in Smith and Yamamoto. *The Beautiful Necessity*, p. 34.

40. Gustav Stickley. "Uses of Wood in the Decoration of the Home." Craftsman Style. www.craftsmanstyle.info/cabinetry/craftsman-wood.htm.

41. Quoted in Todd. *Arts and Crafts Companion*, p. 142.

42. Quoted in Kaplan. *The Arts and Crafts Movement in Europe and America*, p. 273.

43. Barbara Mayer. *In the Arts and Crafts Style*. San Francisco: Chronicle, 1993, p. 86.

44. Darrell Peart. "Greene and Greene Furniture Details," *American Woodworker*, October 24, 2010. http://americanwoodworker.com/blogs/techniques/archive/2010/10/24/greene-and-greene-furniture-details.aspx.

45. Quoted in "Introduction to Robie House Tour Interpretation." Frank Lloyd Wright Preservation Trust. http://gowright.org/MoodleWright/mod/book/view.php?id=59&chapterid=18.

46. Quoted in Mayer. *In the Arts and Crafts Style*, p. 93.

Chapter 4: Decorative Arts

47. Quoted in Todd. *Arts and Crafts Companion*, p. 228.

48. Quoted in Joseph Giovannini. "Design Notebook: Save That Legend! Preservationists to the Rescue." *New York Times*, October 1, 1998. www.nytimes.com/1998/10/01/garden/design-notebook-save-that-legend-preservationists-to-the-rescue.html?pagewanted=all&src=pm.

49. "Louis Comfort Tiffany (1848–1933)." The Metropolitan Museum of Art, www.metmuseum.org/toah/hd/tiff/hd_tiff.htm.

50. Paula Scher. "Dirk van Erp." Design History. http://be-artsy.blogspot.com/p/erp-dirk-van.html.

51. Quoted in Jack Andrews. "Samuel Yellin, Metalworker." *Anvil's Ring*, Summer 1982, p. 8.

52. Anna Fariello. "Samuel Yellin Sketching in Iron." *Metalsmith Magazine*, Fall 2003, The Ganoskin Project. www.ganoksin.com/borisat/nenam/samuel-yellin.htm.

53. Quoted in "Pewabic Pottery." *Michigan Time Traveler*, Lansing Newspapers in Education and the Michigan Historical Center. www.michigan.gov/documents/hal_mhc_mhm_pewabic-tiles_03-10-2004_92006_7.pdf.

54. Steve Fales. "The View from One Hundred Years Grueby." *Journal of Antiques and Collectibles*, May 2004. www.journalofantiques.com/May04/featuremay04.htm.

55. Quoted in Dianne Ayers. "Gustav Stickley's Textiles in the Craftsman Interior." Textile Studio. www.textilestudio.com/article_Stickley_Textiles.htm.

Chapter 5: The Arts and Crafts Revival

56. Quoted in Phil Normand. "Arts and Crafts Ethos in the 21st Century." *Arts and Crafts Messenger*, Colorado Arts and Crafts Society, Spring 2010, p. 2. www.coloarts-crafts.org/documents/CACSNewsSpring2010.pdf.

57. Quoted in Normand. "Arts and Crafts Ethos in the 21st Century."

58. Chris Wilson. "Bungalow on a Budget." *Old-House Journal*, December/January 2004. www.oldhouseonline.com/bungalow-on-a-budget.

59. Quoted in Patricia Poore. "A Bungalow Makeover." *Old-House Journal*, October/November 2003. www.oldhouseonline.com/a-bungalow-makeover.

60. Patricia Poore. "Today's Arts and Crafts Kitchen." *Arts and Crafts Homes and the Revival*, August 25, 2010. http://artsandcraftshomes.com/todays-arts-crafts-kitchens.

61. Quoted in Demetra Aposporos. "A Thoughtful Bungalow Restoration." *Old-House Journal*, June/July 2010. www.oldhouseonline.com/thoughtful-bungalow-restoration.

62. Quoted in "What Is Bungalow Heaven?" Bungalow Heaven. www.bungalowheaven.org/overview/what-is-bungalow-heaven.

63. "Arts and Crafts Design." Bialecki Architects. http://bialeckiarchitects.com/arts_crafts/main/index.htm.

64. "What Is Green Building?" CT Energy Info. www.ctenergyinfo.com/greenbuildings.htm.

65. "Designing Craftsman Style Homes While Sticking to Green Principles." EcoFriend, April 25, 2012. www.ecofriend.com/designing-craftsman-style-homes-sticking-green-principles.html.

66. Regina Cole. "A Handsome 'Green' Foursquare." *Arts and Crafts Homes and the Revival*, March 2, 2011. http://artsandcraftshomes.com/a-handsome-green-foursquare.

67. Quoted in David Keeps. "LA Times Interview: Barbra Streisand Furnishes Her Design Taste." BarbraStreisand.com, October 10, 2009. www.barbrastreisand.com/us/news/la-times-interview-barbra-streisand-furnishes-her-design-taste.

68. Quoted in Bob Brooke. "Tiffany Lamps Fetch Astronomical Prices." *Antiques Almanac*. www.theantiquesalmanac.com/tiffanylamps.htm.

69. Quoted in Mary Ellen Polson. "Three Contemporary Furniture Makers of the Arts and Crafts Revival." *Arts and Crafts Homes and the Revival*, March 16, 2012. http://artsandcraftshomes.com/three-contemporary-furniture-makers-of-the-arts-crafts-revival.

70. Quoted in "The Paragon Dragon Changed My Life." Paragon. www.paragonweb.com/Testimonial.cfm?TID=36.

71. Quoted in "RALA Artisan Listing." RALA Roycrofters at Large Association. www.ralaweb.com/html_pages/artisans_a.html.

Glossary

architect: A person who designs buildings.

art glass: Decorated glass that uses color, texture, and form for its appeal.

Art Nouveau: A movement inspired by nature and characterized by curved lines.

baseboard: Decorative molding at the bottom of a wall where it meets the floor.

beam: A long piece of wood, metal, or reinforced concrete that provides structural support in a building.

cast iron: Iron goods made by heating iron into special molds.

ceramics: Items made of clay that are hardened by heating.

chair rails: Decorative molding on walls at the height of a chair back.

cloud lift: A decorative woodworking design element in which two connecting arcs form a rise in a horizontal line.

courtyard: A patio enclosed by walls that is open to the sky.

craft guild: An organization in which groups of craftsmen employed in the same occupation join together to control the practice of their craft.

design unity: A term used to describe artwork in which the various elements work together to give a sense of belonging.

focal point: In art, a central point that draws the eye into the picture.

Gothic-style architecture: A style that flourished during the Middle Ages and is most associated with churches.

inglenook: A built-in seating alcove surrounding a fireplace.

interdisciplinary: Combining two or more academic, scientific, or artistic fields.

joinery: Wooden joints that connect two pieces of wood.

Middle Ages: The period of European history covering the fifth to fifteenth centuries.

molding: Strips of wood used to cover junctions between walls and floors, windows, doors, or ceilings.

organic architecture: A philosophy that integrates a building's design with its site, furnishings, landscaping, and décor.

settlement house: An institution established in an inner-city that provides educational and social services to people in the surrounding neighborhood.

utopian community: A community set up to perfect some aspect of society.

veranda: A porch or terrace.

wainscoting: Wood paneling or tile that covers the lower half of a wall.

wrought iron: Iron goods made by heating and hammering iron.

For More Information

Books

Carol Belanger. *Authentic Designs from the Arts and Crafts Movement.* Mineola, NY: Dover, 2012. This book presents 406 designs by 80 contemporary artists inspired by the Arts and Crafts movement, which readers can trace or copy.

Charlotte Kelly. *Living in the Arts and Crafts Style: Your Complete Home Decorating Guide.* San Francisco: Chronicle, 2006. This book has information about the Arts and Crafts movement, various photographs and illustrations, and tips on decorating in the arts and crafts style.

Don Nardo. *Frank Lloyd Wright.* Farmington Hills, MI: Lucent, 2012. This book examines Frank Lloyd Wright's life, artwork, and influence on the art world.

Don Nardo. *Medieval European Art and Architecture.* Farmington Hills, MI: Lucent, 2012. This book provides a comprehensive look at the art, architecture, and culture that inspired the Arts and Crafts movement in England.

Kathleen Thorne-Thomsen. *Greene and Greene for Kids.* Layton, UT: Gibbs Smith, 2004. This book looks at the lives of the Greene brothers, their work, and the Arts and Crafts movement with hands-on activities.

Internet Sources

Steve Fales. "The View from 100 Years Grueby." *Journal of Antiques and Collectibles.* (www.journalofantiques .com/May04/featuremay04.htm). This article discusses the history of Grueby's pottery and glazes.

The Louisiana State Museum. "Newcomb Pottery and the Arts and Crafts Movement in Louisiana." (www .crt.state.la.us/museum/online_ exhibits/Newcomb_Pottery). This article provides a wealth of information about the Newcomb Pottery Studio and the Arts and Crafts movement in Louisiana.

The Metropolitan Museum of Art. "The Arts and Crafts Movement in America." (www.metmuseum.org

/toah/hd/acam/hd_acam.htm). This essay provides information about the Arts and Crafts movement as well as a slide show of objects from that period.

The Metropolitan Museum of Art. "Louis Comfort Tiffany (1848–1933)." (www.metmuseum.org /toah/hd/tiff/hd_tiff.htm). This article provides information on Tiffany and his work as well as pictures of his designs.

Websites

Arts and Crafts Homes and the Revival (http://artsandcraftshomes .com). This website is dedicated to the Arts and Crafts movement. It has articles on history, designers, architecture, decorative objects, and furniture, with numerous photos and a large archive.

The Arts and Crafts Society (www.arts -crafts.com). This website provides a wealth of information about every aspect of the Arts and Crafts movement and the artists connected to it.

Craftsman Perspective (www.crafts manperspective.com). This website is a guide to arts and crafts architecture with information about the history of the movement, the different style homes it inspired, and photos of different homes.

Digital Library for the Decorative Arts, "The Craftsman," (http:// digicoll.library.wisc.edu/cgi-bin /DLDecArts/DLDecArts-idx?type =browse&scope=DLDECARTS .HOMEDESIGN). This website provides online copies of every issue of Stickley's magazine dating from 1901 to 1916.

Fallingwater (www.fallingwater.org). This is the official website of Fallingwater, the house Frank Lloyd Wright designed over a waterfall. It has pictures and information about the building, which is now open to the public.

Frank Lloyd Wright (http://franklloyd wright.tercenim.com/index.htm). This website celebrates Wright's work with information and pictures of his buildings.

The Morse Museum (www.morsemuse um.org). This is the website of the Morse Museum in Florida, which houses the world's largest collection of Louis Comfort Tiffany's work.

The Stickley Museum (www.stickley museum.org). This is the website of the Gustav Stickley Museum, which is located in Stickley's former home. Information about Stickley and his work is available as well as photos and videos.

The Webpage of the Roycrofters (www.roycrofter.com). This website is dedicated to Elbert Hubbard and the Roycroft community. It gives historical information, information about the current Roycroft Museum, and links to related websites.

Index

Picture Credits

Cover: © Christie's Images/Corbis

© Bettmann/Corbis, 26

© David Lassman/The Post-Standard/Landov, 97

Desk Chair, Roycroft Shop, c.1905–12 (oak wood), American School, (20th century)/Museum of Fine Arts, Houston, Texas, USA/gift of Isabel B. Wilson and The Brown Foundation, Inc./The Bridgeman Art Library, 61

Digital Image © [1907–1909] Museum Associates/LACMA. Licensed by Art Resource, NY, 56

Digital Image © 1910 Museum Associates/LACMA. Licensed by Art Resource, NY, 80

Digital Image © [1916–1932] Museum Associates/LACMA. Licensed by Art Resource, NY, 52

© Gary Porter/MCT/Landov, 91

Image copyright © The Metropolitan Museum of Art. Image source: Art Resource, NY, 70

© Joe Schmelzer/Beateworks/Corbis, 37

© Karen Melvin/Corbis, 10

© Lara Cerri/Tampa Bay Times/ZUMA Press, Inc./Alamy, 88

© Mark Fiennes/Arcaid/Corbis, 49, 65

© National Geographic Image Collection/Alamy, 76

© Neil Setchfield/Alamy, 41

© Newark Museum/Art Resource, NY, 74

© Peter Harholdt/Corbis, 23

© Peter Horree/Alamy, 67

© Philip Webb/The Bridgeman Art Library/Getty Images, 17

© Robert Harding World Imagery/Alamy, 59, 94

© Romain Blanquart/MCT/Landov, 86

© Science & Society Picture Library/Getty Images, 14

© St. Petersburg Times/ZUMA Press, Inc./Alamy, 83

© The San Diego Union-Tribune/ZUMA Press, Inc./Alamy, 44

© Vespasian/Alamy, 28, 31

© Vintage Images/Alamy, 39

© Walter Bibikow/AWL Images/Getty Images, 34

© William Morris/The Bridgeman Art Library/Getty Images, 20

About the Author

Barbara Sheen is the author of more than seventy-five books for young people. She lives in New Mexico with her family. In her spare time, she likes to swim, walk, garden, and cook. She loves handcrafted objects and Arts and Crafts-era designs.